T0128272

JOURNEY
— TO THE —
TENTH GATE

Life with Guru Gobind Singh - A Spiritual Awakening

KARIN VASTOLA

BALBOA.PRESS
A DIVISION OF HAY HOUSE

Copyright © 2020 Karin Vastola.

All rights reserved. No part of this book may be used or reproduced by any means, graphic, electronic, or mechanical, including photocopying, recording, taping or by any information storage retrieval system without the written permission of the author except in the case of brief quotations embodied in critical articles and reviews.

Balboa Press books may be ordered through booksellers or by contacting:

Balboa Press
A Division of Hay House
1663 Liberty Drive
Bloomington, IN 47403
www.balboapress.com
1 (877) 407-4847

Because of the dynamic nature of the Internet, any web addresses or links contained in this book may have changed since publication and may no longer be valid. The views expressed in this work are solely those of the author and do not necessarily reflect the views of the publisher, and the publisher hereby disclaims any responsibility for them.

The author of this book does not dispense medical advice or prescribe the use of any technique as a form of treatment for physical, emotional, or medical problems without the advice of a physician, either directly or indirectly. The intent of the author is only to offer information of a general nature to help you in your quest for emotional and spiritual well-being. In the event you use any of the information in this book for yourself, which is your constitutional right, the author and the publisher assume no responsibility for your actions.

Any people depicted in stock imagery provided by Getty Images are models, and such images are being used for illustrative purposes only.
Certain stock imagery © Getty Images.

Print information available on the last page.

ISBN: 978-1-9822-3810-0 (sc)
ISBN: 978-1-9822-3812-4 (hc)
ISBN: 978-1-9822-3811-7 (e)

Library of Congress Control Number: 2019918000

Balboa Press rev. date: 06/02/2020

CONTENTS

Dedication vii

Introduction ix

Chapter 1   Steps to the "Tenth Gate" 1

Chapter 2   A Different Stage Unfolds 5

Chapter 3   Big Ego, Big Pain... 13

Chapter 4   Guru Shows Up the Fourth Time 25

Chapter 5   Traditions and Beliefs, Shame and Guilt 31

Chapter 6   The Falcon Visits 47

Chapter 7   A New Way of Thinking 61

Chapter 8   Duality Creates Separation...................................75

Chapter 9   Our Spiritual Evolution 85

Chapter 10 Surrender on a Deeper Level 93

Chapter 11 "L.O.V.E" Is the Wake-up Call............................. 99

Chapter 12 The Impact of Love.. 105

Chapter 13 Seeing the Bigger Picture, Past and Present 109

Chapter 14 "Kundalini Rising" or the "Tenth Gate"
            Opening.. 115

Chapter 15 The Body Is the Temple 121

Chapter 16 We Have Surrendered on a Deeper Level............ 125

Chapter 17 Deeper Insights Still Recovering.......................... 129

Chapter 18 When Ego Disappears... 133

Chapter 19 The "Tenth Gate" Opening Examined Again 139

Chapter 20 Is Daily Life Possible Beyond Bliss?.......................143

Chapter 21   The Energy of God 149
Chapter 22   A New Road 153
Chapter 23   The Experience of Dying 159
Chapter 24   Wisdom Gained 165

DEDICATION

These writings are dedicated to my Daughter.
Without her early wisdom, I wouldn't be here.

My Friends who helped me along the way. I
appreciate your friendship and perseverance.

Souls who helped me along the way, teaching
the lessons I needed to learn most.

All Souls who are yet to come, I appreciate your wisdom.

INTRODUCTION

Spirituality has always been important in my life, but without attachment to any religion. I spent many years of daily meditation inside the Sikh Temple. There was nothing I expected but peace of mind. I loved the daily routine of sitting, focusing the mind, as well as focusing on God, eventually seeing the Universe and the energy in it.

Sitting and contemplating impelled me to become devoted to God. My mind had to become quiet, enabling me to hear and see the things that I write about. That's how Sikhism entered my field of awareness.

During the writing of this book, two important themes became apparent above everything else: One, what we hold true in the mind is how life shapes itself around those beliefs. Two, the mind is the greatest tool, while the body is the temple, they must work together. And in this process, I discovered the soul.

With that I'd like to tell a story. A young elephant was captured. He was to be trained to be a worker. His master had a plan, and this is how he did it:

The young elephant was tied to a post with heavy chains. Thus, he was not able to walk freely, and was confined to a small area. He stayed tied for many years. When he grew strong, his master took him to work. The elephant was a loyal servant.

Every evening when it was time to rest, the elephant had to be tied up again. Now as the adult, and because of so many years of training, his master used a very thin rope to tie him to the post.

The elephant was strong and could have torn this rope in an instant. But by being conditioned for years and years, he did not know that he could have freed himself quickly. He did not dare; he was afraid and not aware. In the elephant's mind he believed he was tied up with a chain.

I tried many ways to become free of pain, because of the beliefs I carried. Some of the things I did to become free of pain included observing people's behaviors, taking classes and attending seminars, related to understanding human nature, but the simple ideas are the ones that stuck. The experiences I write about are simple, but also incredible.

Often, I asked God, "Why do I need this?"

The best answer is I needed to wake up to the present moment. Staying in the moment, every moment. That happens to be the best remedy for uncertainty within the mind, for it creates awareness.

Old, negative patterns of behavior are destructive to people. Without the constant running of the mind, I began to settle down, turning inward. With this insight, I was able to recognize the hidden lessons that brought clarity into my inner life.

The insights I gained have supported me. I see the powerful changes in myself and people who apply self-awareness, while stepping away from old thinking and behavior.

I have pondered many times whether spirituality can be taught or studied. Religion can be taught and studied. That's easy. But how does one explain this phenomenon of experiencing God, and actualizing the awakening of the soul and humbly accepting the presence of God?

For many years I asked how can one explain, during meditation, the life-force in its purest form filling the void within, as the Universe appears before us in its splendor? How is it possible to "observe" God? And by extension, how is it possible to witness the immense concentration of energy, yet understand its benign gentleness. The Universe is the classroom where transformation is palpable. We are living through the expression of God, since everything is perfect.

God, as I have experienced him/her is the perceptive energy that penetrates and permeates, which seeps in and flows out of everything and everyone, ultimately informing me that I am a seed of the cosmos, part of the whole. I am an individual, I am the soul. Humanity is my mirror. The reflections which garner my attention are my lessons. When lessons are not learned, they become my adversary, while ego appoints itself as the gatekeeper of my pain.

In writing this book I always kept in mind that I must consider how consciousness, mindfulness, observations, and beliefs that we carry, play a role in spirituality. What do any of these words mean when associated with spirituality? What is higher awareness? And how does ego play a role relative to consciousness? What are feelings telling us? What part has the heart in all of this? My insight into the heart, spirit and wisdom attained is what I'd like to share with you.

I also write about a considerable force, which I experienced a long time ago. It is called "Kundalini." In the Sikh tradition, it's referred to as "The Opening of the Tenth Gate," or in Punjabi "Dasam Dwar." The energy when awakened brings heightened awareness within the body, increases observation and information to and from our senses. It puts us in touch with our higher wisdom, which I call "Absolute Knowledge." The body is the vehicle that hijacks us into an intense state of ecstasy.

At the same time, the body has lost control, but the expanding mind is propelled into an ethereal awareness. It is here in the realm of highest wisdom, where we collect knowledge through the senses. Perceptions become heightened, they convert into extraordinary sensory perceptions. The body has been catapulted into a world beyond explanation.

When the opening of the "Tenth Gate" occurs, it is the most important event of a lifetime, and the body automatically abides by different laws. Observation is heightened as hyper-awareness overtakes us. We are allowed to comprehend the vastness of the universe and its creation, through which the essence of love pervades.

My wake-up call in the moment was recognizing the endless possibilities of every living human being. Within the body is present a vital force and without it there is no breath, no life. It's the energy of the soul. We must pay attention to the body, physical as well as spiritual. Body and spirit are undeniably connected and what the mind thinks affects the body, what the body feels touches the mind. Both affect the higher consciousness of everything.

With awakening, comes the deepest possible known form of bliss, expansion of the heart, a pass to consciousness and super-consciousness. It brings gifts that are profound: Clarity of mind, focus, and mostly, it opens the path of seeing attachments as the trappings of earthly living. Discipline is the price of admission.

Awakening Kundalini or opening the "Tenth Gate" is a process that can occur unexpectedly, it opens by the grace of God. It's the result of many years of devotion, meditation, breath control, (known as Pranayama) and Yoga. Calmness within body and mind are the essentials. By cultivating these practices, all of us are becoming instrumental in shaping the future of humanity. The awakening to consciousness one person at a time.

I have asked the question if spirituality can be taught or learned. I've had some great teachers, who could only guide me so far. I recognized that my hunger to know God is and always has been deep within me. Ever since I can remember as a young child, I wanted to know God intimately in his wisdom and glory.

In the pages that follow, I intend to share my experiences to the fullest means possible. Mindfulness is the beginning step. Meditation and a focused mind are the guides which lead to profound awareness.

Seeking God is a journey, yet God never left. We arrive when we accept God as the energy which presents itself as godliness in every human being.

As humans we create and destroy. We love and hate. Life is the lesson. We do it again and again until we learn to slow down, become aware, accept, and surrender. We become the observer of the self and watch how the mind wants to control. If we have not learned, we fall into the trap of attachment again. It's the cycle, and it begins with us and ends with our collected wisdom.

When we learn to become mindful, that becomes the foundation of wisdom.

In these pages you may find wisdom repeated, seen from another point of view. Allow the insights to penetrate your soul, the depth of the message is vast and will pass through your subconscious mind in different ways. Wisdom seen from different angles becomes the key to unlocking the hidden self. We allow life to unfold itself, witnessing the self from a higher perspective.

Lack within the heart must be eradicated before real change in mind and soul come to fruition. That's what these pages are promising, a change of view with a wide perspective. The steps are many, it is very much like climbing stairs. Once on top, if we forgot something downstairs, we must walk down again. This is the progress, going back and forth with the stages that we will experience. Repetition, observation and patience are required, but mostly it's a process of unfolding. Enjoy the journey.

CHAPTER 1

STEPS TO THE "TENTH GATE"

THE FIVE VICES

When we live authentically, the five vices are the tools that teach. They are: Lust, Greed, Attachments, Egotism and Anger. To learn about our shortcomings, we devote a lifetime of study to understand why humans employ these vices. Ego is the umbrella that shelters the vices. When we lose ego, we lose the vices.

The five vices are discovered daily through our actions. That is part of our life-purpose: To recognize the vices, to see how and the reasons behind why they fool us, and why we believe in their solace. If we hang on to the belief that they are good for us, they bring pain. Yet, they are our lessons.

The explanations given are my firsthand experiences and not in any specific order. In the deeper wisdom of my experiences, the vices are all part of the lessons, which we will discover throughout these writings. At any point of my experiences one vice or another was involved. Because of the wisdom gathered, the vices are the pearls which I treasure as my teachers.

I discovered the temple in my hometown, because a friend told me about a class on meditation. As I love to meditate, this was the perfect place to hang out for several days with an older East Indian man, who had a lot of world experience. This is how I discovered the Sikh Temple or Gurdwara in Punjabi.

THE TEN GATES

Nine gates are related to the openings of the body and are physical. The "Tenth Gate" is invisible. To explain I'll start on the bottom and work my way up.

My wisdom comes from the experience of the opening of the "Tenth Gate." Everything you read here is experiential. All these openings are basically self-explanatory.

One: Anus.

Two: Penis/ Vagina.

Three: Mouth.

Four and Five: Right and left nostril.

Six and Seven: Right and left ear.

Eight and Nine: Right and left eye.

The back of the head and the crown area is called the "Tenth Gate" and where the opening is experienced.

THE EXPERIENCE

When I experienced the opening of the "Tenth Gate," or in Punjabi "Dasam Dwar," I had no idea what was happening to me. I was amazed after being introduced to Sikhism and reading their Holy Book, where I gathered insights into questions that I had started asking some thirty years earlier. Eventually I had some experiences in the Gurdwara or Temple, which helped me to go deeper into the spiritual journey, which I navigated for many years.

In my heart I am Sikh. I feel as the spiritual warrior, seeking to help souls reach the opening of the "Tenth Gate." The community where I'm now learning from are wonderful people and freely share their wisdom with me. I am grateful.

When I first experienced the "Tenth Gate" opening, I was lost. This was not supposed to happen to a down-to-earth person like me. Besides that, I had no clue what was happening or of its significance.

I searched for answers high and low, but the findings were fruitless. At times I wondered if I was losing my mind. That's how serious my state of mind became. Eventually, I settled in with this newfound energy of highs and lows, which took almost eight years of misery, before I settled down. I had no idea where all of this would lead me.

I'M WALKING BACKWARDS TOWARDS ENLIGHTENMENT

Nothing seems as it appears. In Sikhism there is an idea that everything plays out by stages towards enlightenment. And looking back that's true. But in other ways that was far from what I experienced, never was there a rhyme or reason for what happened. Of course, these are my very own observations and prejudices. Besides, I have not met a single person who has gone through what I did. Only in books have I read of similar experiences as I'm explaining here. But they were also different. So, I figure, enlightenment or the path towards it is sprinkled with many individual pieces and occurrences of one's personal life, and the lessons are different for every person or soul.

What happened to me and at that time of life, I can't say. The one thing I know for sure is this, the "Tenth Gate" opened, I was spun around, as if a cruel joke was played on me. That was more than thirty years ago. However, now I can see how I was walking backwards into the light.

It felt like a big storm had thrown me off a cliff. There I was hanging, trying to work my way up to the top. The top was close, but I was left suspended in midair, waiting to drop at any moment. This event stayed in my body and mind, until I gave up, surrendered, simply because of exhaustion.

For me, there were no precise steps to take, the storm of the "Tenth Gate" came and hit me hard, because it caught me by surprise. It was very unexpected and fun for several months, then it became a downward spiral, with a thrust that hit me hard and nearly put me in the ground.

Eventually, I changed my mind about giving up, and recognized the tremendous energy it brought forth within me. The knowledge I gained is priceless. It shaped how I interpreted my issues that I was waking up to. My problems needed to be seen from a reworked angle, with a transformed mindset and a different skew of light. That was the beginning of understanding for me, shining a different light on everything.

CHAPTER 2

A DIFFERENT STAGE UNFOLDS

THE FIRST APPEARANCE

In March of 2012 I sat inside the Gurdwara (Sikh Temple), during my lunch hour. As always during meditation, my eyes were closed for an extended period. All of a sudden, I felt as if someone was watching me. Of course, I wanted to see what this feeling was so I opened my eyes.

The temple was empty. Suddenly, a beautifully dressed man appeared. I was shocked for a moment. I didn't know what to think. I looked around trying to collect myself. He sat on a large, ornamental, wooden chair. He seemed like a proud man, very much like royalty. He wore a stunning yellow outfit, with a longer coat, shiny yellow pants, and a golden turban with some ornaments on the front, which looked like feathers.

I was confused as he sat and looked at me. "Who is this person?" I thought. Then as fast as he appeared, he disappeared.

Just exactly as one man disappeared, another man entered through the back door. He also wore a turban, which was golden yellow, I stared at him as he bowed down before the altar. This man was not the same gentleman from before. He was a visitor. I was hoping to find a simpler explanation than the one that had been impressed on my mind. "Had I seen a ghost?" I pulled my hair, I had to be sure I was not dreaming.

Within a second it dawned on me, I had seen his picture on the wall in the Langer Hall, (Dining Hall) right above where the food was being served. Quickly, I went out into the Langer Hall to ask or at least get some answers as to who this person is. I was grateful there was a young Granthi (Priest), with whom I had conversations several times before. I asked him by pointing to the wall, "Who is the person in that picture?" "Oh," he said: "This is Guru Gobind Singh, he is our Tenth Guru."

Hearing stories from people at the Gurdwara, I knew the Tenth Guru was long dead. I couldn't tell him what I had seen. It was too fantastic even for me. What I really wanted to say to him was, "Are you sure the Tenth Guru is dead because I just saw him inside the prayer hall?"

I was shocked, literally speechless. Then collected my thoughts, got some food, sat down and slowly began to digest what had happened. Meditation is a way of life for me and have practiced it for many years. In 2002, I had taken a class here at the Gurdwara. It was a good class with ample information and actual meditation. We spent three days sitting, talking and asking questions, reflecting on life and the lessons it may present.

For the next couple of days after seeing Guru Gobind Singh, I was contemplating what to do with this information. I decided to say nothing. At least for now. Even though I had befriended a young man at the temple, who is a Granthi. As a matter of fact, he had been there almost every day when I was there, since 2008. Eventually, I confided in him since we discussed things that might happen during meditation. He asked me what I saw during meditation. That's when I told him about the apparition of Guru Gobind Singh. He believed me.

THE SECOND APPEARANCE

About one week later I sat in the same spot in the Gurdwara. Guru Gobind Singh appeared again. He sat on a chair. He stood up and walked closer. He looked at me to communicate, I heard him say:

"This is the quiet hall. Tell them, this is the quiet hall."

I knew what he meant, he wanted me to tell the people in charge this hall was for prayer and contemplation, not for chatting on the phone or politics or whatever people did inside the hall. Kids had been overly active and noisy that day and were running and shouting.

"This is the quiet hall, and all people need to honor this place as the house of God."

I thought for a moment, bowed my head and said: "Please forgive me Guru, but I don't dare to talk to these men." Would they listen to me, I didn't know? I did not have the courage at that moment to fulfill Guru's request.

In the next instant, before he disappeared again, I decided to be courageous and said: "Guru, I can see you. Guru, I can hear you. Guru, why are you speaking to me?"

"Because you listen."

THE THIRD APPEARANCE

It was another week or maybe ten days later and I was meditating at my favorite spot. To my astonishment, Guru Gobind Singh showed up again. This time, he was very close to me, sitting on a horse. He was tall and with my neck bent backward, I could see him fully from where I was sitting. Still, I moved back slightly so I could take in his whole image with all his splendor right in front of me. The horse was white, but not totally, it was more like a light blue. Guru's outfit was blue like the sky. With a beautiful golden turban that had some ornamentation on the front, close to what it was before. He sat and looked at me. I sat and looked at him, it felt as if time had lost its boundaries and eternity took over. I was awestruck. He was an incredible sight.

His eyes never left mine. I couldn't pay attention to anything else, just his eyes. I was drawn in, while my heart was expanding outward. It felt as if the slightest hint of electricity was running through my body. Bliss took over, all of me was at once electrified and relaxed. Joyful and thoughtful. Excited and calm. Exceptional clarity filled my mind. It seemed as if I was standing on top of a bottomless canyon looking up at him. My heart expanded even more. It was the most incredible feeling. There was no more separation between the physical world and the world where Guruji (as I call him lovingly now) resides. I understood where my path lead in the pursuit of getting to know God in his/her splendor.

MY INNER LIFE

From then on, I knew that Guruji is and always would be by my side. He rests slightly above my left shoulder. Other times he switches. But that means he is telling me something and comes in the visual field of my right eye. At different times, when I ask a question, he will either give me a one- or two-word answer, or not say anything at all because I'll have to figure out life's puzzles by myself. He tells me so.

What he points out is this: Life is composed of experiences, which we create through interactions with people. These exchanges lead to wisdom. My first big message was about beliefs, they are reflected back to me during the process of interacting and communicating with people.

Visiting the Gurdwara was a life-saver for me at those crucial times. Often, I felt controlled by an outside force. Not until Guru Gobind Singh showed up and sat with me in silence did I begin to notice my inner life, or actually paying attention to it. This took many years.

BELIEFS

This is how it works: In the progression of growing from childhood into adulthood, we have taken on behaviors and beliefs, which we live and act by, even when the actions are detrimental to our well-being. At some point, we have accepted what we see in the mirror. In other words, we have become accustomed to being inauthentic, which can be experienced as pain within the heart. This sort of pain is mostly emotional and is not easily seen or diagnosed by a doctor.

To cope with challenges, we tell ourselves a story and live according to the myth. Our creation takes on a whole new way of looking at life. The result is an even more excellent story of inauthentic living. For some people, the story is about shame and the belief it brings. People who have issues with beliefs and most of us do, selfworth will become an issue, especially if selfworth was questioned at a young age. Selfworth or the lack thereof, creates fear, which is the great immobilizer. But it's not easily recognized as such. Anger also plays a role and shows up again and again. Even though emotions are being identified, they may not be seen as the great divide between feeling peace or unrest in an already stressful life.

The great surprise comes when we mature and are finally tired of the same failures and pains experienced, looking to calm an agitated mind and an unhappy heart. Tired of being stuck, we begin the search for answers. The remedies show up when we begin to question and honor our concerns. We may look on the inside for our feelings to guide us in some direction. Feelings are the guideposts. They are the pointers that say: "This is right, this is not right," interpreted by what we feel inside the heart. That is the guide for now.

WISDOM REVEALS – WE ARE BLIND

Beliefs shape everything. If we have the desire to change life, then the mind has to view life from a different perspective. With absolute positivity, when the thinking process changes, life changes. If we're longing to see new and different qualities in the world, the individual has to integrate new behaviors internally. It starts with self-examination and by questioning core beliefs. That's where it begins, within us. We want to experience the outer world differently, we have to change our inner world of old beliefs.

Guruji promised wisdom would come forth. It was in plain sight, sitting in meditation, on the edge of the Universe, seeing all life as neutral energy. The bigger picture became clear, removing emotions from what we believe is happening, creating a fresh understanding unfolding within us like the natural unfolding of a lotus flower. Not one thing is better or worse than another. A problem is only a problem, if we see it as such. Every issue is neutral. If we cannot see it that way, emotions are holding us back with a specific negative belief. This is an opportunity to expand the mind.

As beliefs reveal themselves through the exploration of countless stories, we might not be ready to hear what needs to be heard. In order for the heart to stay open, love is the best remedy, not only for the self, but especially for our Foe. The next insight becomes the acceptance of people who become our teachers, our mirror. They reflect back to us through their behaviors which principles we choose to live, love, or hate by. With this insight, we get a chance to learn and explore who we are on a deep spiritual level.

Practice this point with awareness. Ask:

"Why do I despise some people's actions and judge them?" At the beginning of unlocking what's been hidden, powerfully right in front of our own critical mind, we will not be able to identify "bad" behavior as ours. That is precisely the point of why it troubles us so profoundly. It's bad behavior and it's unacceptable. This is a judgment within us, towards the other. We are genuinely blinded by our own shortcomings. In the beginning of this self-examination, we have no choices. We believe it is an outside source aggravating us.

While still in observation mode, as someone else is acting out, we are the onlooker, blind to our very own judgment and conduct, but easily criticising the one who is showing us the message of what we dispise in our self. Without awarenes, we miss the darkside of the self.

With every interaction, wisdom is laid out, showing us completely who we are at any given moment. Awareness of our beliefs give us an understanding to know what our expectations are of others, but also point to our own shortcomings.

Awareness arrives by observing, realizing the lesson is about my idea of your behavior and how do I expect you to behave in this moment. By doing this, it unveils my own ignorance and the expectations I project unto you.

Take a moment. Visualize what's going on. The teachings are clearly laid out in front of us. Keep awareness in the foreground.

Guruji sat with me for many hours, and his energy brought incredible wisdom and serenity. This helped me to understand that I was blind to my own short-commings. While sitting in silence, looking inward my senses went outward, not to see the world, but deeper to see the Universe, and that allowed me to clearly recognize that illusion and duality are found only in worldly places. The mind when sitting in meditation escapes into a calmness, and when a certain state is reached, enjoys the sweetness of Ambrosial Nectar, (Amrit) that we are allowed to taste only in the silent space, once we reach the single minded space where God awaits us.

BIG EGO, BIG PAIN

Has ego taken us for a ride? Is it possible we are hiding behind a veil of ignorance? Before awareness, we live with deep emotional pain and scars, which trigger us into behaving very unconsciously. Additionally, we judge people and tell our friends how ridiculous someone else's behavior is, while we behave the exact same way and can't see it. The bigger the ego now, the bigger the pain we've experienced as children, the greater the unawareness that still exists.

As adults the ego will react as it always has, with dreadful ways of defending the child who never grew up, and perpetuating the slumber and unawareness, creating more separation from the authentic soul.

As a child I was bullied by adults and peers and did not become skilled in emotional wellness. The ego stepped in to defend me, yet I felt as the victim. I was angry, and did not learn how to exstinguish anger as a child. It really upset me that I was getting blamed for things that were not of my doing. That fact made life even more painful. When I was seven years old, my dad blamed me for not having enough hay for the animals. I had to take the scythe, cut the tall grass and rake it up to feed the goats and rabbits. When there was little water for the goats in their drinking buckets, he became very angry and shouted at me to get the water immediately, or else. Also, I had to milk the animals, but was constantly belittled for never doing a good enough job. I always felt bad about not meeting the expectation of my dad. As an adult I became obsessive about doing things beyond what I felt was good enough. It never occurred to me that I was obsessive.

It takes awareness of the beliefs that control us. How do we gain awareness of what governs us, specifically what triggers us to act with impulsive and or compulsive behavior? A triggered emotion feels like an uncontrollable force taking over and manipulating from a distant location. At that point, we blame the outside world which seems to control us, as if saying: "Look what you've made me do." This creates particular beliefs and keeps us blind while becoming a victim.

One important fact I have to mention here is that my father was an alcoholic. He was brutal when drunk, and out of control. One time I found three kittens in the barn, I brought them to the front yard and played with them. Dad saw me as he looked out the upstairs living room window. He came running downstairs limping because of his prosthesis on his left leg. He carried his hand gun. The three kittens were playing with my shoe laces, while I stood watching them below me. I was extremely happy and wanted them as pets. Dad aproached me, pointing the gun at the kittens. I was bewildered and frigthened, when all of a sudden he turned the gun at me and held it against my right temple. For a moment I thought I was going to die. In his anger he muttered something and turned the gun towards the kittens and shot each one of them dead. Horrified, my mother looked out the same upstairs window and I saw her frigthened face, trying to say something, but no words came out.

When pain is encountered and held in, while not being able to channel it appropriately, anger begins to fester. At some critical and often unexpected moment, anger comes flooding back, because ego needs to act out and protect the child within. We have lost the sense of self. We feel the loss of control. Separation from the authentic self starts at an early stage of our life.

PATTERNS OF BEHAVIOR

How do we let beliefs shape our world? This is a most essential point. We don't realize that the patterns we have established during childhood are still controlling our behaviors. That is until something drastic happens, and that is the moment we need to examine our understanding of life. The question arises: "Why am I repeating specific patterns again and again? What are the answers?"

We create models of behavior that causes discord with our fellow human beings. Worse, it makes us miserable without knowing why. The indicator to see how aware we are of our beliefs is to honestly evaluate the pain that resides within the heart.

TURNING INWARD

Eventually, I became tired, I always felt as the victim. That was the moment I began looking inward. I started to examine my sadness, sorrow, pain, which I constructed with the help of my beliefs, issues I may have met a long time ago, but also not yet resolved. I needed to create stories, which imprinted themselves within the mind and heart as the only reality. The mind and ego constructed a coping mechanism. This is where a lot of my disruptive and self-destructive beliefs stemmed from and it also established some strange idea of expectations to be fulfilled by an outside source.

When no one rescues us we feel powerless, becoming the victim. The attitude seems to be: The world owes us something. Often, people who feel powerless manifest deep and intractable insecurities, that seem to be unexplainable.

There are many different ways that pain expresses itself within the mind and heart. Pain tells us we have adopted a belief that lets us accept we are the victim to the world. In reality, our ego is holding us captive. Which means there is a part in ourselves we cannot accept I call the darkside.

Only in contemplation and meditation, stepping back, observing my self, focusing my mind, did I learn to let the ego induced pain melt away, allowing me to begin to get a glimpse of my authentic nature. The resulting calmness in those moments is raw simplicity in its most beautiful form. Feelings of joy visit the heart and spirit, bringing me back to life.

The next reflection comes down to losing all attachment to ego-driven thinking and reactionary behavior. Once we master these lessons, mindfulness is the result, and as we become free, awareness will be the guide to keep the heart open.

PAYING ATTENTION TO BALANCE

I am compelled to tell a story here. In the last view months, my meditation became shallower, there was a disconnect between the closeness I had felt to Guru Gobind Singh, and the ability to sit still for long periods. I had not seen him for a week, I was wondering why he was not showing up. There was no response. Why was I not heard? After a couple of more days of doubting and examining myself, it hit me like a ton of bricks, Guruji never left. It was me who was too busy to see and hear, or more precisely paying attention to what was happening. I was the one who stepped behind the veil.

However, as I began to question myself, in an unassuming nature, it became clear, I had abandoned my meditation practice without realizing why it happened or exactly when. I simply forgot to think of God and the energy that I experienced as being one with God. When we get caught up in the everyday activities of daily life, we lose sight of what's important. Imbalance in all aspects of life creates stress that keeps us running to from one extreme to the other. That happened to me.

There comes a time in our spiritual journey, when we become complacent. There are many reasons why this happens. Mine was getting too busy with the everyday activities of life, which caused an imbalance that I was not aware of at that moment. Instead of being regular in my meditation practice, I spent a lot of time on extracurricular activities. For weeks I was working more hours, even though I was not getting enough sleep and as a result my health suffered. When I found the time to meditate, I felt as if there were more important things to do and it distracted me, so that focusing became difficult.

Awareness is equally essential as sleeping, eating and meditation, while taking time for contemplation. They are the essential tools for a balanced life. During meditation, the mind and body slow down, the spirit recuperates. We need these timeouts, without them we lose grip on what is real, on what is important and absolutely forget how life in its essence is designed to work on our behalf. It takes awareness to keep the mind open.

What unfolded on my next visit was amazing. I had been stewing in a state of confusion when it hit me, I had given up my wisdom, closed myself off from my friends and family. I was sad and upset at myself. At the Gurdwara, I resigned myself to admit, I had been closed off from myself too. Of course, that meant I could not see or experience any wisdom from beyond myself.

As usual, I sat down, closed my eyes and started to quiet my mind, focusing on the vastness of the universe.

I had a huge desire to see Guruji. I asked, "Guruji please show me something, in some tangible way, I have to know, are you here?" I felt desperate, my mind struggling with doubt.

I expected something to show up, but I had no idea what. Just as I had settled into a nicely quiet mind, I was compelled to open my eyes. In plain view a few feet away a very bright, glistening, beautiful semi-sphere in blue appeared on the carpet. Guruji showed up in a very different way, he was visible to all eyes to see that day.

When I left that afternoon, I was a different person than when I walked in. The cobwebs in my mind were cleared away, once again. The energy I perceived was exalting. Guruji helped to transform the way I could perceive him, and all eyes could see him. Again, I was the only one in that moment who was present with him. This is another beginning of awareness, a different level which I stepped into.

The lesson that day brought home to me was that I have to pay attention to what is happening in daily life, in order to maintain a proper balance. Once on the path, we must be aware and keep pushing to maintain our initial commitment, knowing that it will take fortitude and willpower. The fight that we may experience within ourself, calls upon us to stand up with discipline to maintain our spiritual wellness, which results in bliss, contentment, and balance.

In the next section I will veer away from wisdom of the mind. This part will include how to employ nature to help us.

WHY NATURE

Nature by design has laws. In mathemetics the rules tell us that with numbers we can culculate and measure things. We can create anything with the use of calculation and design. The body's design is very distinct and precise. When we eat, we get waste. When food is consumed, very soon it's converted into energy. Every single action in nature has a reaction. Nature is part of humanity's tool. We use nature to restore our senses. Just as the mathematician has rules to follow, the physical body has rules to follow in order to function properly. The energy-body functions on the same principles and has similar needs. When we ignore the needs of the soul, it cannot express its essence. We get side-tracked.

When the body needs rest, we also have to consider the restoration of the mind and soul. Simply spending time in nature promotes this need. Listen to the sounds of the ocean, birds chirping and water splashing against rocks. The howling wind is a great equalizer for an exhausted mind, just listening can be fun. There are many other ways to restore the restless body, mind, and soul by becoming one with nature.

Paying attention to the falling rain cleanses not only the outside world, but it can also invigorate a starving soul. Swimming in the ocean has a deeply cleansing effect. All senses benefit from the elements. Being in tune with fire, wind, water, and earth, bring peace to an anxious mind and heart.

The process is simple, paying attention and sitting with intention in the elements, while receiving nature without an agenda. Be aware of what nature has to offer, tune in to what is playing out in front of our eyes. Being surrounded by nature brings great energy. In Winter when the sun is missing, we crave her rays to warm a cold body. Thoughtfulness when the body needs healing is of importance. The body and soul thrive on light and sound, which nature provides to our heart's content.

Let nature be part of a daily routine. Sitting on a bench in the park or back yard is a powerful rejuvenator. Walking, breathing, simply enjoying Mother Earth can bring peace to a restless mind.

ENTRAPMENTS AND ATTACHMENTS

The next insight will help us to let go of more ego. Peace of mind rests within the surrendering of it. What else must we yield to? Learning acceptance, since there is no need to have attachments to things, situations or people.

Attachment to "things" is what traps us. The more stuff we have, the more we want or need. Desire keeps us in a state of insatiability. We are happy one moment and the next we are not satisfied. Luxuries give us the feeling of contentment, even for only a short period. That moment of happiness is only a minuscule amount relative to one's lifetime.

When we step onto the train of attachment to "stuff," this creates a severe sidestep from awareness, we lose focus on what's important. We enjoy buying stuff and looking at beautiful things. But is the buying of items a lasting, heartwarming experience? Does it bring us closer to our Creator? Will it bring us closer to us, with authenticity as a reward? What is the need we have to fill? Is there an empty space within the heart, a gnawing pain, that still lingers after a big shopping spree?

Where sadness persists an awareness begins, that enables us to review our assumptions. We can now begin to question everything we hold true as simply an illusion. Attachments and entrapments are illusions.

EMOTIONS AND FEELINGS

Why do emotions and feelings matter so much? Emotions are the feelers or pointers. They inform us from deep within the heart how to view the world. If the world was rough in our childhood, the world treats us rough as adults.

Remember this is a reflection. We behave as if we have a chip on our shoulders. Emotions that stay with us from childhood become impressions of the mind and imprints on the soul. This chip, or attitude is a form of protection and stops us from being mindful towards others and the self. In essence we build a wall. In this way, we are self-absorbed, trying to nurture our wounds, that leaves no energy, creating the lack of self-preservation.

How can we be lacking in self-preservation and have an attitude at the same time? Because we are losing ourselves in turmoil, emotions coerce us, trapping us within the mind, while within the heart we're searching for honest answers. With the wall we have erected around us, we're not able to recognize viable choices that may help us overcome the particular issue that we're struggling with. We blame the rest of the world for our misery. Emotions are powerful, they tell us how we're feeling, while beliefs have overridden our authentic senses. Once we are trapped into believing what emotions are telling us, based on old memories, there appears no way out of this trap.

RECOGNIZING EGO

As we acknowledge to what degree negative emotions influence us with how little control we have over them, another powerful insight becomes evident: Emotions consume us, because they are attached to the ego. Emotions are the fuel that take negative feelings and create disorder as well as expectations of others.

The more we let emotions take over, the less choice we seem to have over them, the greater the pain. As a matter of fact, it is only the memory of the pain that stayed with us from childhood that creates this gap from illusion to reality. The greater the pain (emotion), the larger the ego with which we have to struggle. As we recognize ourselves in the world of spiritual and emotional existence, what do we do with the awareness that our spiritual needs are sorely lacking? And how can we come to grips with our as well as other's emotional pain?

EXPECTATIONS

Sadness exists because we have a specific idea of how people should behave in a particular situation and while in our presence. We have an expectation and the belief that there is only one way of doing a specific thing. It befits us to let go of precise ideas of how people should, could and would behave in our presence. If they don't act to our expectation, we can become extremely judgmental. We point fingers. Where do the fingers point? Back at us when we observe the pointing hand. Only one finger goes forward the rest points back.

It is our behavior that needs altering. Our thinking, when conscientiously observed is just in our head, ego ruling us in how things should, would and could be to our satisfaction. When judgment arises, there is nothing on the outside that needs changing, but our mind and thinking on the inside. Negative judgment hurts people in the process, for it devalues their thinking and behavior.

With an awareness of how we affect people, we let them be who they are, authentic, with their ideas and doings, we allow them to be true just as we can be authentic by taking ego out of the equation and giving up control.

When this lesson is understood, there is no need for ego, no need for control. Authenticity, while living from the heart-center becomes the ultimate freedom and fuels autonomy as strength without ego. This wisdom brings with it an easy surrender, breaking free, letting go of an irrational thinking-process, the belief of having no control. With the promise of surrender the mind rests, knowing that all is well in the world. Nothing has to be controlled, and nothing is controling me.

As this higher insight reveals itself a feeling of openness grows in the heart. The seed of vulnerability begins to grow. Slowly, attachments lose their grip. Control of outcomes cannot exist at this place of being-ness. Living with authenticity from the heart conveys lasting joy. The mind can let go and let God do what God does best, simply being.

BEING VULNERABLE

When understood in full measure, vulnerability becomes the safety-net that surrounds the heart. When genuinely experienced with openness and without fear, it becomes the engine that motivates the heart, letting the heart make assessments, imparting feelings only from the wisdom of the heart, that enables us to surrender to our higher power that dwells within us. When we present vulnerability at our deepest level, we expose the self. Now there is an awareness that alters the mind and changes the body-chemistry, grasping that ego is not present in this moment. Without ego there is no fear, nothing to prove, no attachment to anger or pride or self-importance.

Vulnerability is the sweetness of surrender. Ego with its vices are offered up to reveal themselves in neutrality, no preconceived notions of what's good or bad, just an even flow of life and energy, slowly entering a path of trust and contentment. Control is not an issue anymore. This mind-set becomes the state of invincibility.

CHAPTER 4

GURU SHOWS UP THE FOURTH TIME

The fourth time when Guruji appeared, he stood in front of the altar and was turning in a circle four times. I have no idea what that meant. Since then I have not seen him in human form.

These days he appears almost daily as a hovering blue energy, although in different shapes and sizes. When I'm in meditation or talking to people, he shows up. Sometimes I just smile because he might rest next to a person's left shoulder. How would I explain to an unsuspecting person who is visiting at this very moment?

When I'm in a quandary, I'll ask Guruji to give me a sign during meditation. Then a strange thing happens, my right ear closes, I become deaf to the outside. On the inside, I hear and feel an intense vibration. It seems as if a bird is flying and flapping its wings right next to my ear, a loud whistling noise accompanies this fluttering.

By now I'm used to this energy, it took a couple of times not to panic. Within a minute or so I'm back to normal. And usually, I have an answer. I do not often ask Guruji for any personal advice, but occasionally, I have no choice. Besides, he does not give answers lightly but mostly he is silent. He is present, nothing else matters. In the moments when I experience high awareness, the world is at peace in its entirety.

THE BLUE BEARD

One day when visiting a friend and his wife, they had company. The men were talking in another room, while the wife and I stayed in the kitchen, talking and cooking. The men had eaten before my arrival. During the time I was having my dinner, a strong feeling came over me. I felt compelled to join the two men in their conversation. Instinctively, I walked into the room as if being pushed. I sat on the floor across from them. The men continued talking. Within a couple of minutes, an amazing thing began to unfold.

My friend's friend had a white long beard. Suddenly, his beard started to turn blue in the middle. It looked as if it had been struck with a bright blue light from above. I observed it from side to side, turning my head to see where the blue color originated. I checked the ceiling to see if the light was coming from the top, but it wasn't.

Hesitantly, I said, "Please, can I tell you something?" I had not met this man before and was concerned that he might think I was a bit too forward. "Your beard has a blue stripe in the middle, and now the rest is also starting to turn blue." His full white beard turned completely into a blue hue, with a very distinctive, darker blue stripe across the middle.

The man asked me if I knew that Guru Gobind Singh's favorite color was blue. Of course, I had no idea. It never dawned on me until he said that a Guru could have a favorite color. Now I know.

But it also makes sense, because I saw Guru wearing blue. A beautiful, bright blue. His closest men or soldiers wear blue too, except that blue is much darker.

ONE NOTEWORTHY MEDITATION

One time during an unusual meditation, I stayed at a friend's house for several days. Their family practice is to awaken the Holy Book, Guru Grant Sahib, daily at five-o'clock in the morning. We started the meditation, and four people were in the room when I sat down and closed my eyes. Almost instantly Guruji showed me a picture in my mind, for it played like a movie.

We were sitting in a boat, while Guruji stood in the front. He said, "The five of you who are here with me now will be my first Beloved Ones." I interrupted him and said, "Guruji, there are not five people with you right now?" He responded, "Yes there are."

I argued with him. "There are only four of us here." He repeated himself, "The five of you are my trusted men."

At that moment I could only do one thing, to open my eyes and see if there were really five people sitting in the room. I didn't know the head of the household arrived a few moments earlier, making him the fifth person, just as Guruji said. Astonished, I closed my eyes again and listened to what Guruji was about to say. He said a few words of encouragement. I was humbled. I just watched, while he stood in front of us, his "Beloved Men," and spoke to us in words that gave me a deep feeling of belonging.

We were these five individuals who came together that morning and subsequently a few more mornings thereafter to meditate. But more importantly, in our past lives, we had been with Guruji at the time when he was the "Tenth Guru." He had his "Five Beloved" with him once again. He made it clear to me: "You are the Five Beloved Ones."

In this life we were three women and two men, meditating together and praying. I saw us sitting in a boat, floating in a wide river, surrounded by lush, bright green vegetation, with a giant grey oblong boulder on the land which extended out over the water.

All I can remember is incredible love for Guruji at that moment. On occasions, when I am in company with people from the past, coming together for an hour or a day, I do not ask why. There must be a good reason for these occurences. It's a movie playing in front of my closed eyes, I get to watch what happened in the past, in the present moment. There are many insights still to be come.

God has his ways. Who am I to question? I'm learning many things, just by observation. When I questioned Guruji in that boat, I learned that I needed to trust myself and listen.

AMAZING INSIGHTS

I am gaining in-depth knowledge of many things regarding the Sikh religion. About the people, the wars they fought, and the sacrifices they endured for their freedom and their belief in one God.

In January of 2016, I was listening to a story told by a Granthi at the Gurdwara. The story was about how the two younger sons of Guru Gobind Singh were killed. As I sat and listened a flash of blue appeared in mid-air. Quickly the flash grew larger to the size of a single blanket and spread out close in front of the altar on the carpet. There he was once more. Guru Gobind Singh, visiting.

Guruji stayed for a long while. The dimension of the rectangle changed, it became the size of my hand, floating in midair next to the Granthi's left ear, while he continued the story of how Guruji's two youngest sons were bricked alive. Imagine, a wall of brick was built around them, to die of thirst and starvation.

Within moments another totally unexpected thing happened. Close to where the Granthi sat is a door, it leads to the outside. On the left-hand side of the door a most beautiful spirit with a purple hue appeared, not in the form of a human, but in the shape of an oblong cloud. It was almost the height of the door. Its position was on the left-hand side of the door, as I said. At about the same time a cloud with a tinge of baby-blue color appeared on the right-side of the door. Instantly, I knew they both were the spirits of the older sons of Guru Gobind Singh, the oldest on the left, Ajit Singh, the second oldest on the right, Jujhar Singh.

That was not all. In the next second, two white, twelve-inch diameter puffy clouds appeared. I knew these two were the younger sons of Guru Gobind Singh - Zorawar Singh, and Fateh Singh - they were positioned about two feet next to the second-oldest brother, who was on the right side of the door. Here the story of the two younger boys was told. Their horrible end of life and what they sacrificed for their belief in God, their freedom and the freedom for all Sikhs. The congregation sitting and listening to the horrible story the Granthi told had no idea of their esteemed visitors.

I was overcome with sadness because I could feel the intensity of the gruesome pain inflicted upon the children. However, I also sensed their faith, and the authority they embodied. Their devotion to God was very palpable. The love of the congregation was powerful, I was overcome with sadness and joy at the same time. Everyone in the Gurdwara knows the story of what the sons endured. But I am sure not everybody knew what was happening on a different level of existence.

Again, I did not dare to tell anyone, except a young man, whom I met at the Gurdwara. He is a very spiritual person and knows the Holy Book inside and out. We talked about spirituality and other essential things, mostly about God and related points concerning Sikhism. During his stay at the Gurdwara for several months, I learned a lot. For example, the young man showed me his devotion to God, by examining the Holy Book in detail.

He travelled a long distance from his home literally hundreds of miles, to spend time exploring his spirituality away from family and loved ones, in a different country. Curiously, we had something in common, in that he left home in Canada to search for spiritual insight, and I had left my home in Western Europe, ending up in the same Gurdwara.

He was determined to find answers in his young life. Instead going to college presently, he ended up at the Gurdwara to study and devote time for his spiritual education. He sat and meditated often when I did; I was impressed with his contemplative and unassuming manner, which gave me hope of the resiliency of his generation, who are interested in their spiritual growth.

OBSERVATIONS

One day as I walked into the Langer Hall, I noticed that people's heads were covered, some were not. A sign declared: "Cover your head." I was curious. I decided to ask, "Guru Gobind Singh, why do people cover their heads?"

"It is our tradition!"

So, I asked another question, "I do not cover my head, except here. Does it matter?" Guruji answered again, "Tradition."

He did not say anything else. I just cover my head; it is tradition and shows respect.

CHAPTER 5

TRADITIONS AND BELIEFS, SHAME AND GUILT

What follows in these next pages comes to me after listening to Guruji telling me some short phrases. When I ask, there is always just a one- or two-word answer.

The lessons are a result of contemplation and meditation, as well as life experiences, combined with insights from Guru Gobind Singh. I am compelled to write about traditions and beliefs, because of the tragic results I've witnessed with families who are in total ruin because of old belief systems. My idea is to open channels of communication between parents and children, and people in general.

There are explanations of ideas that may seem far-fetched. As I explain how things evolve, you might find them interesting, looking at life and its ups and downs from a different perspective and keeping an open mind. Most importantly, in my meditation I ask Guruji to help me with the proper applications of wisdom gained.

MY HERITAGE

With traditions come expectations. To fully understand the reasons why and how traditions affect us, it useful to look at shame and guilt, and understand how or why certain circumstances affect us.

I have included some wisdom gained from my experiences at the Gurdwara. During my time spent there, I've had many encounters with people who pushed me to see undeniably what behaviors held me captive to old beliefs and traditions. I also noticed how shame and guilt were tied to my responses while controlling me subconsciously. This was a huge awakening for me.

To appreciate these insights, I'm asking you to step outside of your comfort zone and move to a higher vantage point in your observation of your life. In other words, try to be comfortable transitioning from a simple existence to exalted beingness.

My heritage comes from a very traditional Western European upbringing, mixed with old values and customs from Eastern European thinking. However, World War Two changed a few things, at least in my family. The war was hard on people and they had to compromise themselves and their values. Because of necessity traditions and customs went out the window. But other practices were kept, because of old beliefs.

My family was very much steeped in traditions. Often, I wondered what my parents were thinking when I had to follow some old tradition, like fasting from Friday till Easter Sunday. Or why in Catholic school eating meat on Friday got you a permanent place in hell. Furthermore, wearing a sleeveless dress on Friday was sinful.

The most remarkable and stimulating aspect of learning about different cultures is their view on customs and traditions and how inflexible these interpretations are. Not because they make sense, but because there is an old belief system still in place. An answer given to me frequently was: "Because the neighbors do it, and they've done it for many years. That's why we must do it. Otherwise, we will be less in their eyes." My questioning mind asked: "Are we afraid of being less than the neighbors? So, does that bring shame on us?" What feelings flare up in us when shame is mentioned? Guilt is the perfect companion to shame. We give shame the power to fuel our guilt, or vice versa. The cycle begins.

The belief my parents had adopted was this: By not following a rule of behavior, it will bring shame on us. How does it shame us and why? In my life's experience, there is no real reason why we must live up to someone's expectation of us. However, it became apparent that my parents were enmeshed into a belief system that dictated how people saw them or judged them by way of following a prearranged set of behaviors.

One ominous day, issues I had carried for most of my life flashed in front of my eyes. I took a deep breath, questioned what was happening, and quickly recognized myself as the child who was still burdened as the adult. I surmised the weight carried on my shoulders was a deep insecurity about worthiness.

I did not have many friends growing up. One thing I loved above all else was my alone time. My free time was spent in the forest watching wild animals and collecting plants. Often, I brought home flowers or grasses; my parents had taught me at a young age which plants were good for medicinal teas, or simply tasted wonderful.

The times I spent in the forest taught me to become friends with myself. Loving nature and spending time there helped me to see how it is very healing to the body and mind.

Still, it took years into adulthood to become free of the belief of unworthiness. In many situations I was bullied and reacted to other people's ideas of how I should behave. I believed if I did something for people, they would accept me as their friend. My way out was to be alone and be in nature. As an adult I still like nature, I also learned to like people and have friends without having to earn my friendships.

THE EFFECTS OF SHAME

Living in a tight-knit community, we watched how everyone followed a set of rules. Eventually, we woke up to this fact and began to question this traditional way of controlling society. My parents started to see how a few people made rules, how some people balked at following these rules, and if not supported, being shamed by those who wanted their guidelines strictly adhered to. The lesson is: If we believe their shaming story, we take on the guilt and become the victim.

However, what if we do not give value to the neighbors' ideas and thinking? What if we don't buy into their guilt trip?

To control people, they employ shame as an emotional mechanism that engages guilt, essentially allowing emotions stuck in their head or heart, to affect us. As it turns out, only if we believe in the guilt trip, they direct towards us, will our ego engage. If we don't respond, guilt stays with them and doesn't transfer to us.

It took some years of watching people to comprehend this system as a way of control. I needed more time to grasp how communities and people influence each other. Sitting in the Gurdwara helped me to understand my life-drama.

The credit goes to Guruji who kept saying: "Watch and learn." He didn't say a whole lot more. I figured out by his persistence, this is the place to experience and witness my lessons. "People are your best resource because they are the mirror to your world." And yes, my eyes were opened. Guruji showed me when there is a lesson, we must immerse ourselves in life and be literally caught up, to catch what we're doing and to see precisely why I might be reacting to someone's finger pointing at me. Guru was very persistent. He pointed for me to sit and observe myself and learn my lessons that others are bringing to me. It is a gift for you to have people who are your willing teachers.

After that lesson came another one, even more significant. Observing myself and others, I could easily spot people who carried shame themselves.

Often the way to control someone is to point and make a person feel guilty. It is a sure sign the shaming person is out of control, and not aware of it. They need to hide behind their pointing finger, but in reality it is their own guilt that they are hiding from others.

If we are in a state of reactionary behavior, shame attaches itself to the believer of the guilt trip. Which was me, often reacting to any blame or shame no matter where it came from. However, when we do not respond to other people's guilt refusing to feel shame, their shame and guilt are lost on us and falls on our innocent ears. When their guilt-trip is not acknowledged or verified through a reaction, there is no choice but to keep their judgments to themselves and leave in a hurry, looking for the next victim.

By observing people (including myself) who shame others (including myself), I recognized that through my refusal of attachment to their guilt- trip the hidden becomes apparent. One who establishes his equilibrium which he so desperately needs, by playing with people's emotions and their reactions and not getting a response, moves on to the next victim. One can't get his self-esteem raised by lowering someone else's.

What follows is the account of a young man who learned through listening and observation what was for a while a sad state of beingness. It was a perfect lesson.

Throughout the years I have been fortunate to speak to many young people. When I ask about traditions, they carry the burden of being stuck in the world of their parents as well as their own. Here are two worlds with no obvious choices. When questioned about what they want to do, they hunger for options. The conditioned mind with their traditions, instilled in them a sense of obligation and gives rise to shame. In their mind it is an immense tragedy to bring shame to the family.

Some years ago, I went on vacation. For some reason, the word shame came up again and again. I was watching parents keeping their kids under control by shaming them. At that time, I was privileged to speak to one young man, who was being totally honest with me and confided that he hated the way his parents held shame over his head as a tool to control him. And this is the most crucial part - whenever he had a chance to get away from home without supervision, he would party and drink himself into oblivion with his friends.

His parents never knew. He hid his true feelings very well. He slept his drunkenness off at a friend's house. When he came home, everything seemed well, until the next time. The young man was a closet alcoholic.

He had to hide his true nature from his parents. They were too busy shaming him and later they could not see how or why their son had resorted to alcohol to escape his prison.

All he ever wanted was to be himself, learning a trade and eventually marry and have children. On the other hand, his parents wanted much more for him. They had high expectations. He needed to go to an expensive college, study, get excellent grades and graduate with honors. Because the requests his parents made of him went on and on, he became totally overwhelmed. His parents thought he was wasting his time.

At some point, they realized that something was wrong with their son. It took a lot of time and effort to help him get away from the alcohol addiction.

Eventually, they gave in to his wishes. But shame was still in the picture. He slowly began to understand the psychology of his parent's behavior, especially the mother who herself lived in fear. She had learned from her parents. They controlled her and her siblings with shame. She, being in her fifties still experienced fear of being shamed by her children's failures. She did not gain awareness with age. Her ego again came to rescue the hurt child within. Shame in her life was incredibly powerful. Even with some knowledge, she could not break the cycle. The ego still ran her old emotional pain patterns, for she seemed not able to break free.

How powerful is it then for the son to gain awareness of mindfulness? He learned that his mother had very low self-esteem. He showed compassion for his parents, but at the same time, he began the practice of self-love. In a short period, he understood that he is responsible for himself. He became neutral when his mother wanted to shame him. Shame fell back on her. He could clearly see how shame was her unresolved emotion and she still carried this from childhood.

He knows that shaming is not a compassionate way of relating to people. He has learned that shame is the old way of controlling. In his new way of thinking, he practices mindfulness. Regarding everyone's wishes with kindness and letting people make their choices and then live with the consequences of their decisions.

His parents expected him to become a man, but they treated him like a child. He lived with shame instead of consequences. His parents, mostly mom, was and is stuck in the old way of thinking and behaving.

If he had been allowed to feel the consequences to the full extent, his actions would have been different. Instead, his parents pushed him in a very particular direction by controlling him with shame. He had no choices and was not allowed to make mistakes.

That's why he chose alcohol, he needed to escape. That made for a lengthy detour in his life.

The positive outcome is this: He's learned mindfulness, compassion, a practice of self-love, while he learned to be in-tune with his wisdom. He developed "Five D" thinking (explained later) and looking at life with openness, clarity and deeper understanding of how relationships work. How wonderful is that when you're twenty-four.

Parents have the erroneous belief that if children give in to their bidding, life will be more comfortable. On the other hand, if they don't listen, their actions will bring shame on the family. Guilt does not lay in the child's mind. It lays deeply hidden in the parent's minds.

Shame is maintained still to this day in many cultures with traditions and customs through beliefs. Maybe it is time to let go of control, applying compassion and empathy, profoundly loving and understanding each other as humans, while following a road that was created, on which we follow by the Creator's guidance.

OBSERVING PEOPLE

Recognizing different behaviors in our fellow human-beings is an excellent education. We must understand that problems we encounter in life originate from early childhood beliefs. As babies, we watch our parents and caregivers and we become the sponges through which we repeat our learned behavior. We imitate everything we know until something happens to prove that our belief might be erroneous. And shaming or being shamed is part of these early beliefs.

I ask: "Who is shaming whom?" Was the neighbor shaming my parents, or is it us shaming us because we have the belief that we deserve shame.

Here, I'm inviting you to leap into another place in your mind.

Where are your beliefs coming from? Is it the parents? Did they get the shame treatment from their parents? Are they doing what they know best? In their minds this is the only way to control their offspring. Unfortunately, this is the old way of behaving and raising children. Using humiliation, embarrassment, guilt and shame as the tools to gain or keep power and control. But what happens to the child, who instantly becomes the victim of the shaming game? Sometimes these children become bullies or have a lifelong issue with low self-esteem.

Shaming is a cruel way of relating to another human being. The unsuspecting person becomes the victim and feels plagued by guilt. The connection between shame and guilt is not always noticed and causes emotions to rise, like low self-esteem and inexplicable anger, alongside a profound sense of lack and inadequacy coming from deep within.

Moreover, we might find additional wisdom hidden in this situation. The person shaming us may have an unresolved personal issue and is trying to unload it on us. This is often done to unburden a guilty soul.

Now can you recognize the difference in feelings? Do I need to fix something in myself? When you truly realize that the issue at hand has nothing to do with what has been thrown at you, then you're home free. The person shaming you is trying to unload their guilt. They still believe in their guilt and have not worked out their issues.

IMPRESSION OF THE MIND, IMPRINT ON THE SOUL

When we open our heart and soul we explore and get to know ourselves on a deeper level. To be clear: This journey is to go deep within, because that's where the answers to all life come from - our own wisdom buried deep within.

Back to the point: A guilt trip is being hurled at us.

Someone accuses me of something. The accuser is pointing his finger of shame at me and bellowed loudly for all to hear:

"Why did you do that?"

Because of his unconscious behavior, he manipulates the situation in the form of an accusation caused by his own guilt and shame.

Inside my mind, I step back to take a deep breath and evaluate what is going on in this situation. I say to myself, "Is this situation something I am a part of? Is the trigger something I am part of, or is the accuser merely reacting without understanding what his trigger is?

As we grow in awareness and learn about patterns and habits, we distinguish what's our issue and what's not. We make inroads to explore or at least watch the self, by not reacting and just waiting. In this moment I pay attention to what is unfolding inside of me, I recognize my ego is off the hook, because there is no need respond or to defend my behavior. I have obtained a new perspective through self-observation and by observing other people. As a result, I am observing how the other person's pain is being projected towards me.

When shaming occurs too often when guilt has played out its tune, we know it as a trap set by someone who has deep-seated issues. The one projecting shame on us has not yet recognized himself as being in a deep slumber and can't grasp his/her own innocence.

The one pointing the finger is in reactionary mode, not by choice, but by conditioning. On the subconscious level, they were feeling guilty and ashamed. More powerfully, they believe they are the victim. That makes them innocent. They repeat what they know and what was done to them in childhood. Shame can be pushed toward us, only if we buy into it. Once clearly seen, we can make choices, stepping away from this insanity.

One more point which is of paramount importance. It is at this moment when we clearly recognize that we are still limited by our beliefs in shame and guilt. What is the warning? When we are easily stirred up in reactionary mode, we have work to do.

Eventually, as we wake up, there will be no desire to react. The issues of guilt or shame will have been resolved. Shame happens to many people on many levels. Whole countries live in shame and guilt, for things done in the past.

This insight was a great way of helping me to see how I had been humiliated as a child for things that adults felt guilty about. They had to make up stories to live with their guilt, to unload it on someone who could not defend herself.

Guru Gobind Singh with his persistence kept guiding me towards people who eventually would be helping me, teaching me more of what I desired to learn. Humanity became my mirror. I reacted to shame and guilt until I saw what my consequences have been until this moment in the Langar Hall: I carried a huge burden on my shoulders for things I had no control over but was blamed for as a child. In my mind was ingrained that I was "bad" or "guilty" for something I had done. This guilt had festered inside my heart since early childhood. I was the victim, even through adulthood. As I carried the burden of guilt, the weight was incredibly oppressive on my spirit. The burden brought low self-esteem, unworthiness, depression, and sadness, even though I never fully understood what I was guilty of. Shame is a force; it weighs heavily on innocent shoulders.

Now I understand the shame and guilt I felt. I had no idea why I was often furious with people who laid their guilt trips on me.

The only reason I still bought into victimhood was because of the underlying issues that still worked in my subconcious mind.

I was having lunch in the crowded cafeteria at the Temple, when an old man bellowed at me from the next table:

OVERCOMING THE EFFECTS OF SHAME

"It is not our custom to get up from the table to greet a person!" Which is what I had done, gotten up to say hello to a friend. I understand there may be customs, which I may not be privy to. Yet, this old man was compelled to yell at a stranger whom he had never met before. In the past, I would have been embarrassed or even ashamed. But now I could see undoubtedly, he had issues. He helped me to realize that I did not need to feel shame.

I had carried so much guilt and unworthiness on my shoulders, finally it was time to let go of those beliefs. Formerly if a man yelled at me, I had to be guilty of something. That old man liberated me from earlier wounds of guilt. In my heart, I knew that feeling guilt and shame was no longer mine to bear.

What was the trigger that freed me? I decided to take a deep breath and say to myself: "Is this a situation with which I needed to justify myself? Do I need to react right here and now? No! I was grateful for this moment of awakening.

In that instance I had clarity within my heart, it was him who needed an escape from his bondage to shame and guilt. I just happened to be his trigger and maybe his lesson.

It was my commitment to being authentic to myself, which helped me in this situation. I had no need to justify anything.

Guruji held me to my word, I had promised that I would sit or interact but mostly learn by watching people. His guiding hand was on my shoulder. I shed some skin that day, old skin that needed to be cleared away.

People may not be aware of how shame affects them. We have blind spots with our issues of shaming or being shamed. To project to the outside, seeking fault by blaming others, can be the first - but not always the easiest way to identify - how we are feeling. Shame traps us and keeps us in the illusion of limitation. Shame and guilt will keep us in boundaries with profound limitations that prevent us from living freely. Sadly, this is still a deeply engrained subject for many people.

By paying attention to what's happening with our feelings, of how we react to emotions (our own and the ones projected onto us), becoming hypervigilant, gives us the opportunity not to fall into a dysfunctional and unproductive reactionary mode. Practicing how to respond by slowing down a constantly chattering mind, permits us to survey everything we do.

DARKNESS, LIGHTNESS
ARE THE SAME COIN

The process of reviewing how we react helps us to slow down thoughts and allows stillness of the mind to take hold. Now our priority is to look at our dark side. What is the dark side? It is that which we may not like within ourselves - as a matter of fact, it may be that which we hate about ourselves, although we may not be conscious that it is part of us.

What is dark within, must be accepted. Without acceptance, love cannot exist. In our interest, it's time to take stock, to check in and to ask: How or what am I feeling? Then consider ego's role in this scenario.

Everything we don't like about our self must be examined. By looking at it, we learn to accept it, and learn to love it, as it is a part of who we are and by objectively understanding this, love will motivate us to know our dark side. Maybe not in this instance, but working with ego and all the implications, we understand what triggers us. On a deeper level we begin to feel in this moment what the heart is seeking to express. What do I need to do to stay authentic to myself?

Accepting our shortcomings is a big step to freedom and self-love. Self-love is easier when we practice self-acceptance. By accepting we have a dark side we can begin the process of letting go and believing we are pure of heart. After acceptance, change inevitably occurs, sometimes slowly and for some immediately. By loving the self in totality, we enrich our journey and make deeply profound changes. When loving our self fully, we lose our judgmental attitude, not only towards the self but others as well, because we all have our dark side, but now we understand because we accept.

Occasionally, it is a constructive idea to let the mind go into darkness, and just observe. With an open mind and heart an answer will come from the unexpected place, where the mind may travel.

Always when the darkness is most oppressive, a light begins to shine and brings clarity. Going within to explore and feel one's dark side, viewing one's anger, fear, pride, loneliness, greed, lust and attachment or whatever the dark side may be can be a very liberating experience.

"What do you want, fear or freedom, integrity or being ruled by ego? I want freedom, I want peace of mind, my heart filled with love, being authentic with myself, an open mind, and an awakened consciousness. To attain freedom, being released from the rule of ego, from attachment to worldly things, understanding duality with all its consequences, looking at my dark side and learning acceptance, this is what liberation means to me. On the other hand, denying will send me back to the beginning of doubt and fear, for darkness is fear and acceptance is love.

The first step to enlightenment is understanding that we all have darkness and light within us. Acceptance brings it to light.

EXPERIENCING THE SELF

During meditation a surprising thing happens as soon as the mind is in total silence, suddenly it feels as if the body is separated from itself. Within moments a palpable sensation unfolds. It feels as if cool air circulates on top of my head, I recognize my body is in one location and the essence-self is in another. I am looking at myself from a distance, and there are two entities: myself and the other observing me.

In a moment of revelation, I recognize the "self" being watched by the "self" from a distance. What is this?

In a flicker of a second with the mind in total focus, I have stepped into a whole new world that was safeguarded before, but now reveals a new approach of seeing myself. The veil begins to lift, and an awareness presents itself that subsequently directs me to conscious mindfulness. A different inner dimension reveals itself. A new gate opens.

Behind this gate is the mind in which everything is registered. I become alert to another dimension beyond the values I once profoundly held. The world has not the changed. I float above the "normal" happenings. There is distance between everything I see and do. Like a time-difference, as if life moves in slow-motion. But in real time life still continues in the same fashion. The only difference is, I now perceive life from a different angle, which opens up a whole new perspective.

Old beliefs that once held me captive now become entirely transparent, strengthening my resolve to become witness to the mind in every interaction. Witness means that I step back from

the activity of thinking and I am the observer of the brain, the thoughts, while everything else is in resting mode.

The vastness of the path toward enlightenment means there are many avenues to be explored, and more experiences lie ahead for unlimited advancement towards the awakening of the soul.

CHAPTER 6

THE FALCON VISITS

Late one night I decided to meditate while staying in bed. The friend I stayed with had been meditating for many nights until four in the morning. Then the rest of the family got up and started their morning with the regular prayer and readings from the "Sri Guru Granth Sahib," the Holy Book.

The idea was to join my friend in spirit and meditate together without being in the same room. He is a devoted meditator, we decided this was a great idea.

He was in his prayer room, while I decided to go to bed and eventually fall asleep, but not before joining minds in meditation. I never tried this before and thought it might just be interesting. Before starting, I asked Guru Gobind Singh to help me stay awake. This is what unfolded:

My meditation was intense. I believe my friend and I joined mind and spirit in some universal realm. I saw us flying together. I could see our souls sailing together, exploring the cosmos and God's creation. The Universe with its stars and planets, and other beings were flying with us, as I felt their presence. During this meditation, we were accompanied by many souls. As we entered the realm of deep meditation, all souls can be sensed, because they are gathered within this sacred space.

I can't say how long we traversed the Universe. At some point, I came back to this earthly awareness and noticed that I thought about going to sleep.

That was not going to happen. As I dozed off, a Falcon swooshed right in front of me, flapped his wings and nearly struck me. That is how it felt. I also felt the air generated underneath those wings, and it startled me, so I jumped up. I realized this was not a worldly experience I was having, but a spiritual one.

Immediately afterward I laid down again, getting back to my sleep. The Falcon wouldn't have any of it. As soon as I started dozing off, here came the wings, flapping and swooshing up and down in front of my eyes. Finding sleep with this ruckus was impossible.

I began meditating in earnest again. Soon enough I fell asleep once more. However, as soon as I drifted off, the Falcon kept me company and made it impossible to sleep. This went on all night, till four in the morning. Just as I finally fell asleep, I was awakened by the early alarm, which my roommate had set to get up at four-thirty. She asked me why I had jumped several times during the night and wondered what was happening to me.

During breakfast, I told my story about the Falcon and was quickly informed that Guru Gobind Singh had a Falcon. Now, all the commotion made sense. I had asked Guru Gobind Singh to help me stay awake. What a surprise! I got exactly what I had asked for.

EARTHLY PROBLEMS HAVE LIMITED WORLDLY SOLUTIONS

The soul searches for answers on the spiritual level. The mind looks for answers on the physical, earthly level. Divine answers are found within the divine realm only. To become free of pain it is imperative to transcend emotional issues and seek solutions but without earthly, tangible, emotional ego driven answers.

When seeking answers, mentally step back, slow down the mind. Observe yourself first, look at the problem and then elevate it above human reasoning. Ask: "What would God see?" We must understand that any issue we examine, no matter how difficult, should have a great degree of compassion for the self. The most powerful way in seeing issues is to see them through the eyes of God. Moreover, obstacles are not perceived as such and innocently fall away as we hand our will over to the wisdom of the heart and surrender our mind to God. In a moment of insight, we will understand that difficulties can never be solved with ego, but our essence with its infinite wisdom is forever unraveling knowledge.

FEELINGS OF PAIN

What do painful feelings tell us? A painful experience, for example, can keep us in a quandary for a lifetime if not resolved. My personal experience came from being abused in childhood while under the care of church officials, that left me with severe emotional pain and grew greater because of an unsympathetic community. Throughout my life I searched for ways to eliminate these painful feelings that eventually became extremely negative towards the perpetrators. Pain, for me became the pointers for positive and negative feelings. Not acknowledging a painful matter made it more painful and persistent. They became the "imprint on my soul." As a young preteen child my natural instincts told me something was missing, and my emotions were not valued for what they are, the truth-tellers. As a result pain lingered for many years.

Painful feelings set us up when not attended to, they become the nuisance, the pebble in the shoe, which bothers the foot. We notice but ignore it. At first, it's just an irritation. Soon we try to tolerate. Eventually, feelings become severe emotional burdens, and profound suffering sets in throughout the entire physical body. My whole personality was affected. My heart ached, whenever I recalled those traumatic experiences from my childhood.

Pain, in the beginning, can be emotional but transforms into physical manifestation. Although it may not be felt from the heart or that region, however, when asked, people report aches coming from the heart area.

What creates heartache? While the heart and the soul are connected, the soul always seeks to express who we are in our deepest essence. The soul is deeply touched by emotions and when we cannot express our desires and feelings the heart experiences pain, so our humanity, our spirit suffers. When in pain the body and mind demand increased attention. Sooner or later we must take care of their needs.

RESOLVING THE PAIN, THE JOURNEY BEGINS

As I began to understand how the pain affected me, I began to understand the need to address it, I recognized a restlessness in me that needed to be tackled. It was a restlessness that resulted from not fully resolving those issues when I was a little girl. Starting when I was a teenager, I consciously resolved to start on a spiritual journey of self- understanding. By then I had read a lot of psychology books from Carl Jung, Sigmund Freud and others. In my thirties I took classes and had therapy sessions with counselors and facilitators who specialized in childhood trauma. I discovered what it meant to be authentic with the self, that an anxious mind, ultimately craved to be heard.

The brain looks for different ways to escape. It runs itself into a state of helplessness. The result is a run down and tired mind. It is overwhelmed and in this state no clarity can exist. If the exhausted body is not capable of finding an efficient way to rest and relax soon, it will see itself in a dangerous downward spiral. For some life becomes joyless and burdensome. I found this to be true in my life, but throughout all of this I always felt that God never left me. Now I became a seeker. I undertook this journey with the knowledge I would never look back. The pain I experienced as a young girl became the pointer that guided me to expand my spiritual horizon. I understood that although you don't need to endure the pain, it can become a life-long teacher that guided me to eventually healing the painful soul.

TAKING CARE OF OTHER NEEDS

Time to take stock. If you're not sure what is going on, tiredness can play tricks on the mind, life can become overwhelming. Taking timeout for meditation, the mind needs silence to recuperate. Talking to friends or a counselor can also be very helpful.

In my early thirties as my spiritual quest continued, I sought to practice various models of therapy, and in so doing I obtained certificates that certify I was an accomplished Reiki practitioner, Japanese Massage practitioner, with restorative massage. In Thailand I learned Thai massage. I studied with Clarity Institute in California, and at the same time I became a Clinical Ayurvedic Specialist, and eventually practiced Ayurvedic Medicine with my clients both East Indians and Westerners as well as Europeans, in Germany and Austria.

Despite the accumulated knowledge of the healing profession I still knew within my heart, my healing was only on the surface. My life was extremely hectic and consumed with taking care of others. I needed to take care of myself.

Letting feelings dictate is often best. At the beginning of the journey to awareness, spending time alone to rest and relax, without having to perform or do any work is best. I relied on intuition, hoping to find different ways of letting the soul and body recover. Foremost, being kind to the self is of great value. As a spiritual seeker, it is of importance to sit back, with an open mind and heart, and let happen what may and merely watch life float by, without assessment of what is being witnessed. Just pure observation. After a while, it becomes clear that feelings are the pointers.

LET YOUR FEELINGS BE YOUR GUIDE

What are your feelings telling you? Feelings provide the wisdom. Emotions and feelings are the sensors which are bursting forth with information that exceeds the obvious five senses. Within the range of the "normal" senses, humanity has reached its boundaries. The constraints are coming off, there is more than physical confirmation of who we are. By seeking out the spiritual realm, we turn toward an all-embracing expression of the spirit we once were, thus helping us to remember what we have been missing.

A beautiful way to let the body, mind, and soul relax is by creating a space for expansion in all three aspects of the "self." The body and mind need rest, with extended periods of silence. Giving the mind a rest will bring unexpected wisdom especially when there were moments of crisis, that causes the mind to act in panic. That space for expansion delivers answers that would be impossible to be received otherwise, except in this state of conscious stillnes. As the mind is learning to let go of control, the soul is seeking answers in the realm of the soul, which is the only place where unlimited solutions are presented!

In such silent moments, thoughts become unmistakably clear. Stepping into the soul realm, emotions and feelings become transparent. This recognition looms over us because we are indebted to long held emotions, feelings and beliefs. This is the time when we can go beyond the sense perceptions of old thinking and behaving. We are shedding old belief systems. The mind seeks out freedom, by being in stillness. Every insight turns out to be the restoration of the heart, which includes the healing of ego and intellect. We acknowledge the mind as the "gate keeper," the one requiring wisdom. Ego is the "pain keeper," the one requiring trust. The heart is the "wisdom keeper," the one requiring only love for the self. Our senses are the "broadcasters and safety keepers" of the body, that when attended to, tell us everything we need to know, because now the veil is removed, opening the way to be in tune with ourselves.

The wisdom we seek is about the self, and how we can become closer to our Higher Power, we call Creator or God. On the spiritual journey we may begin to see how we are the ones who created limitations. How did we end up with this overactive, emotionally stunted mind, that leaves us often with discomfort and pain? Question and examine these fundamental issues again, including your personal belief systems, awareness of your inner-most feelings, for they are the instigators of the roller coaster ride you may find yourself on in your life.

As we uncover our emotional obstacles (while seriously studying them), recognize that the senses are not what we thought they are. This opens us to the wisdom we seek about the self.

Through the practice of silencing the mind with deep meditation we begin to see life from a different angle. As we experience the influence of solitude, the mind carries us forward into a deeper spiritual level, and our outlook changes. We are able to step into a different vision of life. As our vision unfolds, life is always about the attitude of how we perceive the world on the inside, and the outside world must follow suit. A limited mindset will provide us with a limited worldview. And the opposite is true. What you think is what you get.

In one of my meditations, I had the desire to be totally unburdened by the everyday activities of life. My day was extremely hectic and I was glad to be invited to a gathering in which I felt I could relax. I longed to feel a lightness and ease in my body. I stood and closed my eyes. A bright light arrived immediately. Usually it shows up later. Since I was standing, I was aware of the people sitting close by who were also meditating. As the light became brighter, it was as if the sun was glowing through the clouds. I could not resist and opened my eyes, I had to see where this bright light was coming from. Amazingly, it was still cloudy and grey outside, but the light was so bright, that it forced me to close my eyes and surrender into it. This surprised me, but I was ready for whatever came next. This was when I lost all senses. I did not exist in that moment of time, and my conscious self left. I felt extremely free of all constraints, brought on by daily stressors.

The feelings I experienced during this meditation went from lightness to super lightness to a realm that I cannot explain, except that I felt a vast expanse of stillness open up before me. I stood for thirty minutes. Part of my super-conscious mind was taken to another realm. Afterwards, I realized I had experienced an unexplicable, yet unconscious state, which I never forgot.

MORE ON IMPRESSIONS
AND IMPRINTS

Why are emotions so powerful? Everything that happens in life, emotions are part of the essence of human development. Without them or the understanding of how emotions shape us, and how emotions operate within the mind, our spiritual growth will be stunted. The impact of emotional wellness informs all parts of our lives.

In childhood everything we experience is a lesson. Some moments are fun, other moments turn out to be life altering. When teachings are handed out in unkind ways, the ego takes note. People who may be our parents, family, friends, teachers, and strangers may act in cruel ways towards us. Unless these behaviors are repeated, we tend to forget. However, if we encounter harsh or unjust treatment, as part of a routine, the memories become part of the emotional war chest we accumulate. Ego shows up and grows stronger and stronger.

Unbeknownst to the child, he/she, collects these abuses within the memory bank of the mind. The hurt feelings become stored emotions and are "impressions of the mind" and if repeated become "imprints on the soul."

The more frequent these feelings leave impressions on the mind, the more profound the imprints within the soul become. Years later as adults, when someone acts out or speaks to us, which may or may not remind us consciously of something from childhood, we are caught off guard. That memory comes forth and most likely we don't remember who, what circumstance, or why pain was created. Depending on the feelings triggered, the more powerful the reaction, the more significant is the pain we feel.

The pain we experience in moments of triggered discomfort is the ego stepping forward, protecting us as it were. Ego is also that part of the mind which at any given moment, especially if triggered by old memories, pipes up and wants to be heard. Ego needs to be understood and vindicated because of old unresolved feelings, which are imprinted within the soul. Ego demands an explanation; it needs to be heard and its demands rectified. When the body and mind have endured pain, ego is the fixer, or so it appears.

CONQUERING DOUBT, THE LESSON OF THE WALL

In the beginning, when entering the temple, I felt a sense of belonging. My search to find God was not inclusive of organized religion. I've attended many churches, Buddhist or Christian, I respect all religious beliefs, but to belong to any one religious philosophy is one's personal choice.

Even after experiencing the opening of the "Tenth Gate" I had no idea where my spirituality would lead, I was impelled to continue to search for a spiritual truth about my very existence. As I continued my search, I also experienced how deeply soul searching it can be.

For example, one particular day, as I stepped through the doors into the prayer hall of the Gurdwara, I felt a "wall," like a membrane that I bumped into while entering. It took years of walking through this layer, until I recognized it was the layer of ego I was bumping into. This layer was so unusually impenetrable, I even felt it when I bowed down in front of the altar. I had to make an effort to release this layer and surrender to it. This was not an easy lesson and it was intense. I had an unresolved doubt that needed to be released, which was a secret I unconsciously kept since I was very young. It was my doubt about organized religion.

I struggled for the longest time, Guruji helped me to understand this unresolved doubt was my own ego. He pointed towards this big lesson, and directed me again to people and circumstances I could watch at the Temple, because they reflected back to what I did not fully understand about myself. Now when I bow down in front of the altar, there is no layer I bump into. The practice of devotion to God and the release of ego is finally softening me up.

WORTHINESS AND AWARENESS

Believing outside judgments of our worthiness and by means of other people's opinion, may result in giving away our soul. This is old thinking. Instead, make it a priority to know the self as the soul with a higher consciousness. And with this wisdom, life shifts again. So many erroneous beliefs keep us enslaved to emotional, irrational thinking. We gave our power away through beliefs and emotions which were deeply ingrained, and we suffered grievously. We now realize, by not taking responsibility for our actions, we took on the victim persona.

We judged so easily, but now recognize that all judgments are sentences against the self, and so we put judgment aside permanently. By being accountable for our behavior and actions, we become the master of our destiny. We are now waking up to our divinity. This soul has existed, and will be, long after the physical body is gone.

The imprints of the soul are turned over, by releasing ego from its duty as the keeper of pain, we now learn to exercise our senses as the pointers and use emotions as a guideline for our highs or lows. The trappings of old emotional, reactionary behaviors no longer control us.

As we become experts in self-observation, we also become experts in observing other people. This state of consciousness is a different way of seeing and experiencing life, which enable us to step away effortlessly from reactionary feelings and behaviors. We see humanity as the equalizer. Everyone is the soul first, the body is second. We are all the same. If we're engaging in struggles, we may have a chance to escape; our newfound mindset gives us the opportunity to wake up, recognizing our divinity.

As soul we know with certainty there is more to life than earthly desires. With this certainty in mind, we begin a journey towards a limitless life, with emotional clarity as the cultivator, planting the seeds, that will sprout and carry us closer to the Creator. We thus witness ego as the principal teacher. Life will have meaning and worthiness when ego becomes our friend and not the enemy.

New traditions create new experiences. From new impressions, new beliefs and values are created. Everyone has life-experience and grows from it. Every human being is developing new skills and evolves on his/her terms, based on personal maturity. Authenticity will rise to every occasion. When love for the "self" is generously instilled within the child, as well as the adult, there is no need for feelings of unworthiness. Separation from the Creator cannot occur, because we have gathered awareness and through this awareness no separation exists.

In the Sikh spiritual writings, we find many sacred guidelines of Universal truths.

"SACRED NITNEM"

Fundamentals of Gurmat, writings from the Sikh Holy Book.

> "18. *The true place of pilgrimage and the true temple exists within the man, where Divine Nectar and Light exists, covered by the curtain of ego.*"

Sukhmani Sahib
"(vii) *He must abandon ego and the self.*"

We experience life through the colored glasses of ego. Our sensor of how to navigate life is an old emotional wound. Ego is that which demands attention, when ignored it rears its ugly head, anytime anywhere. Once we seize the darkness within, the light shines brightly, and we become liberated from ego. Then ego becomes our servant as it is meant to be.

Divine Nectar begins to flow within by developing an attitude of gratitude and devotion. While we learn to appreciate each being as the soul first, considering our own fantastic creation through God, we find love for ourselves. Then the light inside begins to glow.

This is achievable by silencing the mind, by living a life of total devotion to the Creator. Letting ego melt away with the rest of the world. The inner light will emerge, it is our birthright. Once the light begins to shimmer, it is unstoppable. It informs the cosmos that we are ready to receive "Divine Nectar." (Author's note)

CHAPTER 7

A NEW WAY OF THINKING

EXPLANATION OF "3 D" TO "5 D THINKING"

In my old way of looking at the world, I used to think of life as clear-cut and I accepted without questioning the accompanying baggage, that is life happens to us, instead of us creating life. When things didn't work out well to my satisfaction, I sought someone or something to blame, pointing outward away from me. Essentially this scenario is what I call the "3 D" thinking, and the subsequent "5 D thinking," from which this part of the book will endeavor to explain. By not letting the reader know this and because of my experiences, we can become a victim (as I was) and not be aware of it.

"3 D THINKING"

I believe "3 D Thinking" is like being stuck in a box. Three surfaces: Length, height, and depth. We behave in the old ways, impressions from long ago have locked down the mind and are still running the show.

Now in a new millennium, many people I personally know (like myself) want to walk away from burdens, illusions, being trapped in a cycle of life, that for one reason or another, seems foreign and inauthentic, not of their own making. Despite philosophies, theories, religion, moral codes, etc., I notice a good portion of the people are still not satisfied with their lives. It seems to me the "sins," (the beliefs) of their parents and older generations, are still defining their lives. However, humanity is growing in the awareness that old ways of behaving is not working anymore. Entrenched values and traditions do not necessarily inspire new ideas to come forth from the depth of one's soul.

As I look at the world within my generation and their concerns there is no doubt that new concepts and understanding of other-worldly ideas have been accepted in this generation. Being in a spiritual community of like-minded people doesn't expose one to ridicule anymore, however the deeper spiritual experience of the individual is often not fully appreciated by a wider community. This individual is often alone and daunted by this tremendous spiritual experience and growth. This has been my personal experience. From this I constructed the "5 D" thinking upon which my whole spiritual life unfolded. The result was that it gave me the opportunity to go further into a personal spiritual reality.

ADDING DIMENSIONS TO EXPAND THE VIEW

As we add several more components to our thinking, we create greater capacity for space within. By doing so, we eventually leave our comfort zone and the rational mind behind. The mind is strong, given the fact it has been conditioned since childhood.

Experimentation with slowing down time can be practiced. Thereby learning to combine aspects of ether and time, while allowing us to step into a different element created within the mind. The compassionate heart will be the ultimate guide, as we practice a different way of seeing our world from the inside to the outside. Whatever we believe on the inside, we will get to experience on the outside.

TIME AND ETHER

I suppose what I did was I discovered time was not linear at all like a stream flowing, being accountable only to the principle of gravity. Time could go backward as well as forward, it could be stopped. In my meditation practice I also knew the ether is where God resides. I discovered that time and ether comprised the two dimensions which compliments the other three, which gives me the awareness that the mind expands far greater than I previously thought. Time is a construct that benefits us because we are learning to guide it beyond a known boundary. This boundary included that I was able to stop linear time and look from above as if I was a spectator being able to experience the movement of time and the stillness of time.

Time is an integral part of the universe. Time, as the way we understand it with a twenty four hour cycle is not what is important here. To be more accurate, time is not separate from seconds, minutes, or even hours. No, everything exists all at once.

It is inevitiable that time will come to meet us, however we have to be perceptive enought to hold time still or to let it flow beyond us. It is also a basic truth that the construct of time is not necessarily an illusion but it is as real as the air we breathe. My observation of time is this: When I observe time and have an expectation, like speeding it up or slowing time down, that is what I witness - a speeding up or slowing down. This means to me that when I watch time with awareness and intentionality, I get what I want.

Years ago, I became concerned that my regular meditation was not enough anymore. I yearned for a closer intimacy with God. During that time I went to the Gurdwara sporadically. Within a few months I found myself at the Gurdwara daily, sometimes twice a day. I invited friends to the Gurdwara instead of to the movies.

As time went on I felt a shift in my way of thinking and it dawned on me that my understanding of time had changed.

The first lesson for me became the awareness that my heart was closed off with fear or worry. I needed a pracitice that included daily meditation, but what I really longed for was to get to know God more intimately. My regular meditation was not enough anymore. At about the same time I started to go to the temple every day. I began a devotional practice, by thinking of God as the only thing that mattered, also by doing my work with enjoyment. Everything I did was important, and I learned to do it with pleasure.

One morning as I drove to work I experienced what I call a time-shift. That's when I realized time is not as linear as it seems, because it was altered in front of my eyes. I sat at the red light and waited for a long couple of minutes. In my mind I began to wonder what was going to happen next and I think I said out loud: "I wonder what will come next?" Within a second I saw a white car pull up on the opposite side of the road. In my backview mirror I saw a red car pull up right behind me.

In the meantime my light turned green and I drove off. As I drove onto the freeway via the ramp, there was no red car behind me. I turned my head and looked back, as a red car sped towards me. That was my first time when I thought that something strange occurred. The next morning I did the same thing again. I was at the same light as the day before, waiting to get on the freeway at the intersection onramp. I asked in my mind if I could see what was about to happen before it actually occurred. It happened again. In the rear view mirror I saw several cars behind me, but when I turned my head, there were no cars. I knew I was on to something. From that morning on I played a game and became very skilled at seeing things happen before they actually did.

That was not the only game I played. I made an effort to see things that were further away in time, like what was going to happen next week. That worked too. But I felt uncomfortable doing that. I had a feeling as if I was creating Karma for myself. That is the last thing I wanted to do.

Early in the morning, I began my meditation. A short time later, after meditating, I opened my eyes and watched the air around my orchids move. It seemed as if the air was hotter around the plant and moved in waves, approximately one inch around the plant itself. This happened early in the still of the quiet morning, no heat was present. It was the ether that moved. Time slowed down for me to see the movement of the ether. My mind perceived the ether in slow motion.

At some point I remembered that years ago I had experienced the ether moving. What I mean by that is when I am in a certain state of mind, I see the air move, like the phenomena of a mirage in front of my eyes. Later it dawned on me after the Kundalini experience some thirty years ago a very similar thing happened. As a matter of fact I saw the air move in front of me quite often and later just forgot about it. Now that I'm more aware of these things, I feel that in this time of my life some of these experiences are coming back, especially during meditation or right after. I treat these occurences with more respect. I also realize what happened to me when the "Tenth Gate" opened is still affecting me. The experience of Kundalini or the "Tenth Gate" opening will always influence the way I see life. Because of this experience many years ago, I have gained a whole new way of approaching life. For instance, my approach to meditation has become very focused.

I also realize as I'm writing this book, I was unconsciously trying to remove the Kundalini effects in my life, but utterly failed for I just did not understand either out of ignorance or fear how these changes truly impacted me. I can see now how in so many ways they have expanded my earthly existence and as a result I appreciate that all existence have multiple dimensions beyond everyday human consciousness on this earthly plane. One final note, in trying to understand the impact of how our human experiences may not be fully appreciated because our lives are slowly developing and as yet not entirely focused we may overlook certain things that were significant in our life and may not see them as a continuum leading to greater spiritual awareness. A simple story is in order.

I was busy as a young mother making a living as a massage therapist, working for a high-end spa. I had a friend who was a Blackfoot, Native American who needed work done on his knee. As he was not the typical clientele but rather simply dressed with well-worn clothing and humble in his demeanor, he caught the attention of my boss who felt that I should not invite him to come to the spa, since he obviously did not look like the our regular wealthy customers.

I politely told my friend about my boss's request and my friend replied, "That's fine, I understand." Then he said: "I have a gift for you."

He aked to me sit down on the massage table and close my eyes. I waited as he pressed a finger on my forehead and I heard a fluttering noise as though a bird flew by my right ear. He asked me to open my eyes and when I did, I looked at my left hand that rested on my knee. What I saw astonished me, there was a bright, radiating, pulsating, wave of transluscent, emerald green that grew bigger and engulfed my entire hand as well as my knee. From that day on I could clearly see intensely colorful auras on people, trees, rocks, anything in nature.

Little did I know that as the years followed this and other experiences were preludes that lead to the opening of the "Tenth Gate."

"5 D" APPLICATION

How do we step into "5D" thinking? Here I feel it helps to quote from the "Sacred Nitnem."

Chapter IV
SUMMARY OF THE TEACHINGS OF JAP(U) JI
3. Stanzas 1 to 3: How to achieve eternal bliss and Perpetual Union with the Creator. How to destroy the wall of falsehood which separates the human soul from the Supreme Soul.

(i) One must obey and abide by the will of God. Which has all virtues and powers of God Himself.

(ii) Realize that the will of God governs and controls the entire creation. None can interfere with His will.

(iii) This will is the cause of the world drama, and people may go on describing and narrating it, it is impossible for anyone to describe the same.

4. Stanzas 4 to 7: Penance, charity pilgrimages, etc. are useless – meditation upon God and worship enable realization. By developing deep love, "higher consciousness expands."

5. By hearing the name of God and meditating upon Him, most valuable gifts are received.

To the earnest seeker of God, wisdom and truth reveal themselves when we meditate on the Creator. To understand the will of God and what that means, we must leave old ways of thinking behind, and old belief systems must be entirely relinquished.

When we let go of the drama and the theatrics, we create the life we were meant to live. Ego is the ulcer; it festers and creates drama.

It keeps our mind harried by feeding us fear, separation from God, unworthiness, or any such thing related to low self-esteem.

The gift of seeing the "self" through the eyes of God, opens the heart to the core and radiates purity thus resonating unity with love. Developing deep love within is how higher consciousness matures, where separation from God is impossible. (Author's note)

HOW "5 D THINKING" EXPANDS OUR VIEW

Old beliefs will have to be abandoned, especially the ones that kept us running like a squirrel in a cage of "3 D" living. Now as we stand on top of the box and look out to "5 D" (remember "5 D" includes time and ether, and "3 D" includes height, depth, and width) we can see the old belief systems crumble, while recognizing the illusions, the fear, and the unrealistic expectations that we were brainwashed to believe. Now we recognize that everything that happens to us originates within our world. Stepping away from the "3 D" box changes our attitude because by looking at life from a different and higher vantage point, we develop a broader perception, changing our view of life.

Adjustment starts with the mind. Resistance creates pain held within the mind and heart. Our experiences (emotions) present themselves as struggle. We fight and kick, we carry on a battle, while struggles inhabit the mind. That is the drama we have created, and this story repeats itself over and over.

This is the valuable lesson: It is to identify the drama and leave it behind, and we do this by looking within the heart with repeated examination until we firmly understand what we're feeling.

Resistance can be strong, yet it is not complicated. We experience it as discomfort, or pain. It pushes on the inside trying to get out. It is ego with long standing issues, leaving the heart stagnant, filled with perceptions of unresolved issues, as it pushes against our will. It is the ego that pushes us, needing to be right. The ego still wants to be in control. Unrecognized resistance within the self is very strong, but it can be lessened and eventually stopped.

How can we stop the resistance that creates a dysfunctional life? Only in surrender, only in acceptance of ego can resistance pass through our unconsciously self-erected wall. This is possible only with the knowledge and awareness of seeing ego acting out within the self. Then letting ego surrender with our own kindness, giving up easily the power-struggle within the self. The wall of pain disappears.

Ether is the space where God exists. Because ether is omniscient and omnipresent it allows us to move from one level of existence to a different one, wider and deeper in scope. Witnessing the self bestows us the ability to expand our horizon and indeed step above the ego-centered being-ness and watch from up-high how life offers up choices.

It is at this level, we become alert to ourselves in being aware and present. Watch, observe and discover the place where God exists. Within the ether, there is no resistance to anything, where ego cannot exist. And finally, with stillness in the mind, we can witness the self from a different vantage point, wisdom is present, and God can be heard and seen.

UNDERSTANDING MINDFULNESS AND MEDITATION

When I practice meditation regularly, I experience radical transformations. Worries, fear, anxieties, and other negative emotions dissipate with time and practice. Science is recognizing that different areas of the brain develop different ways of processing challenges. When meditation is practiced a change in structure within the brain occurs. We can improve processes within the mind that calm the brain, help to eliminate fears, even go as far as to understand illness in a different light, and train the mind to respond differently to the body affected by disease. A mindful attitude can heal the body.

Meditation is a tool for mindfulness. When we apply this tool to its fullest function, it will transform our feelings. It will improve our mindset, which then enhances the body chemistry.

Breath used consciously is the ultimate gateway to the body and mind, helping to transform the nervous system, teaching us to deliberate our actions before we dive into reactions.

With the practice of gaining insight into our mind and heart, we ultimately connect to a force greater than our self. Therein rests the profound mystery of breathing, sitting still, focusing the mind. Once we learn how to concentrate and understand where our focus is directed, that's where awareness grows. When we focus to improve as well as enhance all aspects of life radically, we change our entire physiology and psyche.

We can overcome old trauma, stress, lingering addictions, eliminating old beliefs, conquering loneliness, understanding the self with greater compassion, while developing empathy. Most powerfully, we cultivate self-love and acceptance, creating a well-rounded, healthy personality.

We are creating a whole new persona. The old self is there but infused with insight. The activities involved in a practice of meditation and mindfulness are not hard, yet they take time, effort and a daily routine. Once we have entered the realm and heard the voice of God, seeing the Universe in its totality, catching a glimpse of what it means to be "One" with the Creator, everything changes.

Following are some daily practices, helping to establish a happier more wisdom-driven life.

BEING GRATEFUL

A daily routine of gratefulness is a beautiful way of starting out in the morning. Saying "thank you" in the first three minutes of waking up. Being in awe of the miracle of life and the time we are given on earth to appreciate how wonderful life is. Thanking the sunshine in the morning, or having a soft, comfortable bed. Be grateful for all the little and big pleasures that make life incredibly perfect. Gratefulness lightens the heart and brings happiness. Feelings of gratefulness transform into grace.

GRACE

When true grace is experienced, our emotional behavior changes on a deeper, more visceral level. True grace enhances your emotional well-being and elevates your spiritual growth to a great degree. Unnecessary emotional drama loses the capacity to hold us captive. The cellular memory in the physical body is seriously affected by this change, therefore also affecting the emotional body. Benevolence shines through as an imprint on the soul. Generosity of spirit takes over. The energy body as well as the physical body manifest themselves with deeper compassion for all sentient life. The soul is deeply touched by grace.

BEING HAPPY

After practicing gratefulness, grace takes over. And before we know it happiness seeps in from the heart, to occupy the rest of the body, while the keen mind searches for more reasons for gratitude. Happiness cannot be stopped. Abide in it, and let it take over. Happiness is a journey, with many hills, valleys, and bridges to be crossed.

LISTENING

With meditation we are intently seeking God. The truth is, God never left. We have forgotten God. We stopped listening, which is the most obvious part of communication. We are asking the mind to be silent. Only in silence the mind expands. We must become vigilant in our actions, above all vigilance in our thoughts is of great significance.

Understanding this helps us in any situation where communication just means that it is time to sit still and listen in silence with an open ear and heart.

Listening implies that some other person is present. Listening can be the most significant gift we can offer to a friend in need. Judgment and opinion stays out. Listening is an action, but nothing is required, just an open ear and heart.

When we listen to a brother or sister, we hold the space for them to be heard and to express anything that may be close to their heart. We offer our ear, listen with an open heart and let them be who they are. This is a most precious treasure.

When we listen to ourself we listen also to our negative feelings. The amount of energy we use to ignore our negative feelings sets us up for emotional upset. When emotions have taken a toll on our health it is our duty to address the issues at hand.

Emotions have powerful energy. Depending on how long this energy has been ignored, it may manifest itself as a heavy heart and often a sense of desperation accompanies it. Acknowledging this insight helps you to become aware of all energies and the fatigue they can create in your system.

Often issues that can't be reckoned with are placed back on the shelf, meaning we want to forget them. Yes, there are issues that can be overwhelming. However, with the ear of a trusting friend, we can place our expectations in proper perspective. Unfortunately, when not addressed properly, they become the giants we begin to dread. Taking the time to look at issues is important. Facing our fears is part of the emotional, spiritual journey.

From German lore comes a saying: "Face your pig." "Seh deinen inneren Schweinehund an." This means we must look at what we fear and dread. The sooner the better. Placing what we fear on the backburner does not help. Emotions take energy but when we examine them, they'll convert into positive action.

CHAPTER 8

DUALITY CREATES SEPARATION

Please read the following before starting the lesson, since it will make more sense.

Imagine we're in a meditation setting. We now silence the mind with focused breathing. Eventually, calmness must follow. Initially, we are aware of our surroundings and then we are aware of our internal response to this practice. Then superficial self-examination of our behavior takes place. Next comes the stillness of the mind.

To understand duality and how to appreciate its value, we must observe the wandering mind. To most experienced meditation practitioners, the wandering mind is an impediment to achieving the stillness of the mind. However, I have discovered (surprisingly, many others who also meditate have discovered the same), the wandering mind is simply part of a duality that we want to discover. Keeping in mind not to worry as this is part of the process.

Over the course of decades of practicing deep meditation, I experienced there is a significant point during the meditation process in which the stillness of the mind definitely dominates the session. It's the point before the stillness of the mind that I would like to discuss. And this is the crux of this theme.

A long time ago as I was sitting in a meditative state, when a powerful thought hit me. Meditation is not just the silence within, but it is the noise outside too. Before the stillness of the mind, the mind is in conflict.

The duality is at this point a manifest reality that reveals itself. Conflict, mind-chatter, and stillness of the mind are accepted. After surrendering to the conflict, the mind opens and quiets itself, thus the stillness inevitably takes over for a prolonged period of time which supersedes the mind-chatter. Soon the stillness of the mind dominates.

Just as when we surrender and then accept the feelings of negative emotions with the body, we begin the process in the physical healing and the same happens to the mind in meditation.

At one point a certain awareness sinks in, we are content. The mind was not wandering. No thoughts penetrated the brain. We're happy, still and calm. At this point, we then appreciate the value when we were not still and calm, for we already have surrendered and accepted its impact on our psyche during the course of this meditation session. This happens as a result of recognizing that the stillness can only occur after the mind chatter. The quiet mind and the busy mind are like day and night. This stark contrast is impossible to avoid and it is absolutely experiential.

The question must be asked: "How can one listen to the voice of God when the brain is too busy being in many places all at once?"

The first Guru of the Sikh religion Guru Nanak Dev says this:

"A restless mind knows not the way."

How can we think clearly when the mind is racing, the heart is beating, and we're running in four different directions all at the same time? Our desire for peace or contentment eludes us.

We are beginning to wake up to the fact that there are two aspects to our meditation, the calm and still part that brings contentment and the other part that we want to get away from which is restlessness. We are in a restless state of mind most of the time. We have clearly recognized duality and are able to step back and watch these two opposites come together within the mind.

Reading for practice ends here, please practice a simple meditation and see what awareness will come first.

Writings from the Sikh Holy Book.

The Pauree II says: *The self-willed manmukh (a person who exhibits no humility, love, no contentment or spiritual wisdom), wanders in duality, lured and enticed by duality.*

When we are distracted by duality, we have lost ourselves. We suffer because of duality. Without awareness of duality, we cannot become conscious, thus separating us from the Creator. Be still, focus on God and look deeper. Eventually, duality will show up for you to recognize. (Author's note)

BECOMING THE WITNESS

After duality is observed we may also observe or more precisely, we recognize an awareness and this awareness presents us with an awareness of another self. This might happen in a blink of an eye. It is possible only when we truly witness the self as we sit and watch and become aware, there is more to me than just one. I watch my body; my actions and my thoughts from afar. But who is this one looking at me from beyond myself? Here is my higher self, becoming aware of me, beyond me.

Through this new transparency, can we understand how duality, excitement, and calmness, must come together to teach us mindfulness. But also, the mind lets us see more of itself. We recognize within a nanosecond some other "thing" is playing out. Once we study duality, there is more to it than meets the eye. We see another duality playing out, there is me and there is my "other me." We clearly witness our self as two, as witness we look on as we recognize the body as being separate from the mind, with several feet of distance. The body feels smaller than usual.

As this experience unfolds, I witness everything from a higher vantage point. I'm floating above, while my physical body is walking ahead of me. A feeling of bliss and lightness accompanies this event. After several minutes, sometimes hours, this event subsides, and I go back to normal. It brings with it a feeling of weightlessness, as if I could fly in such moments. We become the witness to the self.

FREEDOM AND CHOICE

The path to greater spiritual awareness is not always easy. At times obstacles may obstruct our freedom and our choices may appear to be limited. This view of mine was made clear several years ago as I was leading a meditation session, when at the end we engaged in a discussion about what we think or how we feel about a particular topic. I brought up the idea that we are limited in our choices. One of my students voiced her opinion: "We all have choices." While I understood the underlying thought behind her thinking, I felt it was necessary to expand the student's understanding of conscious awareness in the choices they make as they progress in life. Needless to say, I suggested a point of view with an illustration. The illustration is of a prisoner who sits in a cell with four walls around him and he is scared, depressed and lonely, with no one to help. Does such a prisoner in this situation have a choice? One's spiritual quest may put us within the walls of a prison-like situation, and we may feel that we have choices that seemingly gives us the opportunity that we may be free of this prison-like bond in our life. Because we, when not aware of our choices are conditioned by the mind, and that overrides our inner spiritual wisdom.

When we have life-long conditioning of the mind, our choices are only based on those conditions. The mind cannot see any other choices except what is ingrained since childhood.

Some years ago, I lived the American dream, married with a decent life, and a daughter. At some point everything fell apart and I was presented with an obstacle. I remember sitting and reflecting on my entire life. How it had all come to this point, it occurred to me I had no choice but to continue playing the role of a single mom struggling to make ends meet and wondering if this will be my lot in life until the day I die. It seemed that life was a series of dead-end possibilities without any positive outcomes. Whatever choices that were before me none of them seemed to be available because of the weight I had to carry.

When my daughter who was eight, came home from school one day and complained that there was no food in the fridge, and we had no money to buy groceries. After paying the bills, I had no money left for food, because the money ran out before the month was over. I was cash poor, so I had to come up with some idea to feed my daughter and me. Right then and there I decided to pray about what I could do. This is what unfolded. I had a dream that impressed me so powerfully, I had to follow it.

I saw myself selling sandwiches in the office complexes in my neighborhood. As a matter of fact, I saw the little alleys, roads and office complexes laid out for me in a plan. When I woke up, I knew I had to follow this plan exactly as dreamt. I had to prepare and by the end of a month, I was fully committed and was able to gather all the necessary ingredients to make healthy sandwiches. Immediately, I set out to find the office complexes I saw in my dream. Everything unfolded as in the dream.

The Sandwich Lady was my daughter's choice for the name of the company. In a short few months customers were plentiful, and I acquired a commercial kitchen in which we not only produced sandwiches for wholesale but made breakfast and lunch for over seventy-five employees who worked for the company that provided my commercial kitchen on the company's site rent free.

When we're not aware of the mind's ability to overcome seemingly impossible situations that tell us there is no choice, we are in a prison. Not having a choice is a conditioning of the mind that imprisons us. And for many it is absolutely a reality.

We have relegated ourselves to be dis-empowered, simply because of our mind conditioning. Choices we make can be made with the help of a consciously unobstructed effort from the depth of our spiritual wisdom. Our own fear which holds us prisoner must be relegated to an illusion. Spiritual growth depends on our inner strength, which when applied produce supernatural results.

CONDITIONING OF THE MIND

Our conditioning begins when we develop impressions of the mind and imprints on the soul. Beginning very early in life we may experience adverse situations, and these are filed away within the mind. Some situations cause feelings to become impressions, some are not, depending on the sensitivity of the person. The longer an impresssion lingers, is repeated, or coupled with a traumatic event, eventually becomes an imprint. For example, it may not be outwardly apparent why we fear darkness. The ego wants to protect us, imprinting this memory within the soul. We unconsciously revert to old behaviors.

Many years ago, I saw how this characteristic affected a friend of mine, when we were at another friend's house. This woman invited us to her bedroom, because she wanted our opinion as she was trying on new clothes. We stayed there for a long time, until we got hungry. The friend decided to let us stay at her house, while she went out to the neighborhood deli to get some food.

Since my friend got a little bored, she began looking at her friend's other outfits hanging in the closet. We both happened to be in the closet at the same time, when my friend inadvertently closed the closet door shut, and when she tried to open the door, the handle separated from the door. Of course, she realized the door could not be opened since the handle was now disconnected. The room was dark, and the light-switch was on the outside.

My friend had the biggest panic attack I had ever seen with an adult. She was deadly afraid of the dark. She screamed like a child. I could not console her for the longest time. A few minutes later when her friend came back from the deli, my friend was still in extreme panic mode.

In that moment, she could not figure out why she was so afraid. Her fear of darkness made absolutely no sense. As a matter of fact, in that instance she was looking to blame me and her friend who had nothing to do with being locked in the dark space. Her mind was on lockdown, no choices. More importantly she lost her freedom. Whatever happened to her at some indeterminate time in her past caused her to relive the trauma in the present. The imprint manifested a dramatic physical and emotional response that left her unable to understand.

After we got out of the closet, she suffered for several more hours. I observed her, she wouldn't talk much, except to stammer and blame. Today that incident or her reaction would be called PTSD, post-traumatic stress disorder. How many people have suffered abuse as children and are suffering today from those emotional wounds? I see many closed off people who have shut down their hearts because of abuse. If no change happens, their ego will protect them for a lifetime.

This may not be what you have experienced, but memories of punishment or abuse are shielded within the heart/soul. Until the moment when there is a trigger and the old memory lurches forth with pent up anger, negative emotions or old and stuck behaviors are unleashed. Do we have a choice at that moment? No, the victim is ruled by the experience of the past.

Every single feeling experienced throughout life is stored as imprint on the soul. Although we might feel emotions coming from an external source, these feelings linger deep within us. When someone points an accusatory finger at us and we are triggered, emotions within well up. Once this becomes apparent, we recognize the old imprints and understand that beliefs are ruling us.

By practicing awareness we can step away from those illusions. On some occasions, the ego will step in, when the need for control is felt by the mind. Again observation of the "self" is of importance, and there can be no judgment. If we fall back into a clouded mind, we want our "will" to be done. Let it be. The old patterns want to react, even if just for a moment. Thank yourself for the ability to witness the old habits, as they pass on for good. Always ask God for more wisdom.

The notion of opening the heart and letting more humility guide us now can be fully anchored into the mind. Say to yourself: "God, help me to open my heart even more." Then be still and feel deeper, feel what wants to come up, listen to the inner voice, because it is your heart that speaks. What will it tell you? Can you see yourself as divine, powerful, gracious, and the generous person you are? With more practice of deep breathing, focusing on the loving heart, grace will envelop your being-ness, in time the heart will open energetically.

When I practiced opening my heart to myself and paid attention to how I felt, I observed the energy within me was more expansive than I realized. It became clear to me that love energizes the body and the past negative impressions are released, for with love there is absolutely no pain. With mindful consciousness, I was free to make the choice to rise in love with myself. It seemed that I was able to let go of a certain rigidity I had felt for many years, which was like a barrier around me from the outside world. I felt like I could relax, which I didn't experience before.

All these feelings began to resonate inside of me, identifying that I am responsible for all the walls around me, and that offered me the power to release them. The powerful rigidity of the walls around me crumbled to the ground. Vulnerability now becomes a strength. When resistance within is recognized as the wall, which I had equated to feeling safe, that became the insight that reinforced losing attachment to it.

CHAPTER 9

OUR SPIRITUAL EVOLUTION

"Real spirituality demands that we take a step towards that which we reject." Llewellyn Vaughan-Lee

Recently, I spent an hour of meditation at the Gurdwara when an unforgettable and extraordinary experience played out right in front of my eyes. It was at the end of the day when the Holy Book is put to bed. This is a tradition in the Sikh religion. Just before this happens, the Granthis are singing Kirtan or special hymns. Like the voices of harmonious angels, they sounded so beautiful. I closed my eyes and was swept up by the sounds. The music and singing went on and on. I became incredibly moved by the melodies.

When I opened my eyes, I saw Guru Gobind Singh in front of the altar. He appeared in his usual blue color and rectangular shape. Within moments the image in front of the altar grew into the most intense, bright light I had ever seen. It was as if the deep blue ocean and the brightest sun had merged inside the sacred prayer hall. The light and reflections were beyond belief, as the brightness forced me to close my eyes. The faces of the people sitting nearby glistened with astounding intensity.

Several times I opened my eyes, but the power of the light was too intense. It's hard to explain what happened next. I began to question what I was seeing. My mind asked: Is this really happening, or is it only my imagination? Instantly the brightness of the blue and the glistening of the sun began to fade. I realized that I was doubting what was happening and this caused the beautiful phenomena to slowly fade. This was a startling revelation. Right then and there I resolved to leave any uncertainty or doubts of the reality that Guru Gobind Singh is unquestionably present. Within a second the light became bright again. In front of me was an "ascended being," showing me the light show of a lifetime. I am honored to witness his presence, I am honored to see the light.

The message made a huge impression on me. When I doubt, I change everything. Guruji showed me without hesitation when the mind questions, when ego takes over, everything is in a state of flux. But more importantly, my faith and trust I had developed, my devotion to God and Guruji, was in question.

The inner workings of my ego changed everything. Why did I question myself and doubted? Why did I lose faith in this moment? With absolute clarity, I saw how faith is necessary for a deep inner spiritual life. It required that I must have complete trust and clarity.

As we progress in our spiritual evolution, perceptions are heightened. Ideas of how human-ness is evolving are questioned even more. There comes a moment when you recognize that your soul has a greater authority than your ego, and that the soul and the ego have traded places. This is a great awakening. My soul was liberated once more from the rulership of ego. This different way of seeing myself brought me the gift to make spiritual and ultimately behavioral changes in ways I had not imagined.

WISE LIVING

Take responsibility for your actions.
Take responsibility for your thoughts.

Stop being offended.

Let go of your need to win.

Let go of your need to be right.

Let go of your need to be superior.

Let go of your need to have more.

Let go of identifying yourself by your achievements.

Let go of your reputation.

Be kind to yourself.

Be kind to others.

Have no definitions about yourself.

How you see and treat yourself, is how you see and treat the world.

In return, the world will treat you, in like manner.

Practice empathy, kindness carries you forward, it sets you free.

To surrender, let go of your will, for it facilitates breaking free of weaknesses and old habits.

Surrender equals freedom.

Love yourself first. That is the beginning and the end of all wisdom.

WISE WORDS TO LIVE BY

Take responsibility for your actions. As we gain knowledge of the self, we develop confidence, believing that life will work out. However, if we let doubt slip in, even for just a second, we lose clarity. Trust demands that we take responsibility for what we're thinking and by recognizing how often we permit the ego to merely take over; this causes some erroneous thoughts to create fear in us. But within this moment of recognition, it becomes clear there is a choice to be made. Don't walk in fear but trust the higher self. Furthermore, take responsibility for every single action.

The next step is: Do not take on a guilt trip. We are not being offended. The only way we are offended is when we are either guilty or ashamed of something and reacting because we have gone back to past behavior. Being offended corresponds to becoming the victim. We have no reason to be offended when we are striving to become spiritually and consciously aware people.

The need to win is a sign of lack within the soul. The need to be accepted is also a lack and can become an obsession. This soul has never experienced abundance as a child, was criticized often, never received a gift purely for enjoyment, and without attachment of an expectation. Most likely this soul was teased as a poor performer. His or her contributions were never recognized, never listened to and not understood. It is also possible this soul was always rescued by an adult parent or grandparent. Possibly too, this soul never had to be responsible for anything and was protected from any deliberate work and chores. Presenting this soul with the gift of acceptance is essential. They need to practice acceptance of and for themselves. Letting them take responsibility for everything that comes their way, while at the same time letting them feel the consequences of their behavior, will help them to accept greater responsibility.

The need to be right is a lack of seeing oneself as intelligent, not able to speak as a child and tell their story. Deep insecurities accompany this soul, they were most likely teased and misunderstood, and not allowed to voice an opinion. Their intelligence was not valued, at least in their mind. A parent or caregiver may also have rescued this soul continuously, without allowing the child to take responsibility for any of his actions. There may have been a power struggle with a controlling parent.

The need to be superior stems from the lack of seeing oneself as brilliant. Every human has abilities, gifts, and talents, but not recognizing these could have been instilled due to lack of parental guidance. Adults did not listen or pay attention to this child. Inadequacy is felt within the heart and is transferred into adulthood. Victimization plays out in this person into adulthood and the need to be superior came from adults who may have told the child that he was dumb and provided no outlet for free expression for the child's benefit.

The need to have more. It is more important to recognize that our spiritual needs may compete with our inordinate desire to obtain more material possessions. Are we living happily and with contentment? Often, when we feel enough is not enough, the ego rules our sense of abundance or the lack thereof. When the need exists to have more, enhanced by mindful greediness, life becomes heavy with stuff for more than what is needed. This thinking creates pain.

Identifying with achievements. It is a person, who when they were young, was not acknowledged or accepted for his being-ness, who always had to show something, in order to feel valued. The parents and peers conditioned this mind to such a degree that they began to believe that they were nothing without tangible achievements. Thus, begins a cycle of identifying with achievements. Only with a high degree of achievement is this child valuable, not only to himself but, he believes the outside world needs to see him with big achievements. This soul can't grasp the concept of being cherished for simply being human.

The same goes for having a reputation. Identifying oneself for having a reputation can result in living up to both a good and bad reputation. Eventually, this "thing" becomes so engrained that pride shows up. When self-importance takes over, ego is in charge. Having a reputation can become very exhausting. That second skin is always there. The true personality cannot reveal itself. This human is wearing a mask and has to live up to a false image of himself.

Be kind to yourself. What does it take to be kind? Letting all pretenses fall away, loving the self unconditionally, without hesitation and in any circumstance.

Be kind to others. What does it take to be kind to others? Letting all pretenses fall away, loving the other unconditionally, without hesitation and in any circumstance. Treat people how you would like to be treated and give more than what is expected.

Have no definitions about you. In the beginning of your spiritual journey, if you've formed a definition about yourself, you have already made your spiritual path difficult. A person with no definition of himself is open to criticisms, either constructive or destructive and yet is able to distill the essence of the intent of the criticism. A person who has no definition of himself is sensible enough to allow humility to lead his way of thinking.

It is a wise idea not to identify with earthly things. That includes diseases, wealth, or other things that make or break us, as we link these ideas to our spiritual well-being. Once connected, we become these things. The mind believes what the emotions deliver.

How you see and treat yourself is how you see and treat the world. Treat the world right and the world will treat you rightly. This statement is by no means passive. We can honor others by realizing that we treat them as we want to be treated. It implies effort and action for the good of others. Our actions must be positive, with the implied affirmation of deeply held beliefs and with love as its foundation. We treat others as we want to be treated.

By practicing empathy, kindness carries you forward setting you free. In daily life we encounter many people; walking in their shoes shows empathy, feeling their pain opens the heart for more kindness. When judgment is gone, we become free to be more vulnerable to show our humanity on a more profound level. When we express empathy for humanity, love shines through.

To surrender, to let go of your will, facilitates breaking free of weaknesses and old habits. To surrender the will is of paramount importance in the quest for seeking spiritual wisdom. The reason we're seeking wisdom is to let go of preconceived notions. Yes, but are we willing to let totally go of our ego-driven knowledge? This is one of the most powerful lessons and is learned after many years of trial and error.

Ego can become our friend and can relax by letting go of control. When ego steps back in humility, the mind has finally realized it is not the victim, everything is in divine order. The limitation of always having to be right falls away. Old habits have no more shape to suspend us in some made-up story of drama and trauma that we were once addicted to.

Surrender equals freedom. When there is no identification with past, present or future outcomes, no beliefs to tie us down, when ego is letting go of the mind and resting in a state of openness and vulnerability, we become free. We sit with equanimity. Life is good.

Love yourself first. Love is a natural thing. When our heart fills with love and understands that we are love and love is to be given away, this removes all obstacles from the mind. It wipes clean our old beliefs, it clears up fear, hostility, and anger. We must develop love for the self, for without it we cannot exist in a spiritual way. Humanity can not move forward in its spiritual evolution without love. The energy of love can be felt as much as electricity can be felt.

Once the energy of love is felt and understood, it changes our outlook regarding everything and everybody. It opens the heart. It shows us that we are all the Beloveds to each other. All doubts are left behind. Furthermore, we are able to see the world as our playground, to explore and to care of it as our Beloved.

Love is the beginning and the end of wisdom.

CHAPTER 10

SURRENDER ON A DEEPER LEVEL

What is surrender? In the dictionary it says to give up, to yield, to relinquish, lay down, to turn in.

Simply put it means to give up something. In the spiritual sense what does it mean to give ourselves up? First, we can give up resistance to the way we see the world. Accept how life plays out. Resistance can be felt if we pay attention. A very specific feeling accompanies when we can't accept an issue in life. There is an energy that surrounds us when we resist. What do we yield to when silence is required? What do we give up when we are in a struggle?

We might fear anything that's new, which then gives rise to resistance, and is felt within the body. Surrender means giving up the energy that stands between us and peace of mind. It's pure energy we give up, once we surrender. That frees more energy for other things in life.

Only in a silent moment can we begin to bear the fruits of our struggles, therefore enabling us to find an answer if we listen. Opportunities lay in the surrender of the moment. Our Creator has a chance to shine through the clouded mind. Are we ready to hear and give up control? We sit with awareness, with neutrality, with no preconceived ideas of what comes next. With the focused mind, emotions no longer distract us. We observe within, seeing directly how precious gifts have eluded us. Leave all doubt behind and recognize that doubt is the big hindrance of our spiritual evolution.

Life becomes filled with thoughts of intention, with a new relaxed and natural way of experiencing and noticing our outward behaviors. More importantly, we validate our inside behaviors, finding that this existence we call life is congruent with what we feel on the inside and how we perceive life on the outside. Our life is now touched by a vulnerable innocence that was ours when we took that first step as a child.

Profound happiness takes its place in the heart. Detachment has come to guide us. Surrender leads to humility. Emotions that held us captive are now distant, they don't matter anymore. In its place a childlike openness has replaced intolerance. Love continues to expand within, and what follows is the natural expansion to the outside world. In our reflection of love, we recognize divinity in all beings. At some point there will be no need for reflection, we will embody our divinity and manifest it. We surrender and energy begins to flow.

LEVELS OF EMOTION

One more reason to meditate and contemplate is that all our senses become incredibly refined. We find out how emotions are the gatekeepers that informs our life. There are many levels of emotions. For example, we experience one kind of pleasure for an extended period of time, for it gives us joy. One day something major happens that brings greater joy. From that we gained the ability to feel different degrees of pleasure. All emotions, positive and negative have different levels of expression.

We intuit this, but it may not necessarily register within the cognitive brain. While in meditation or maybe just in a moment of silence, we can clearly and naturally see how we are attached to our emotions. When emotions and feelings dominate our meditation practice, the tendency may frustrate our goal of eventually stilling the mind. Remember that emotions have different levels or degrees. To effectively still the mind, removing emotions or feelings may not be possible all at once. Therefore, it is better to remove them by degrees, little by little like removing the multi-layered skins of an onion.

Meditation has other challenges for the beginner. This might include emotional issues that occur while in silence as when the mind tries to remove all thoughts. For many people such thoughts as emotional trauma or unresolved issues are difficult to remove. This is natural. This is often the result of us wanting something and not getting our wish fulfilled, which causes us to feel upset. And in that moment, we become sad or mad or even angry. When this happens, it is a sign that we are attached to something outside, that either brings us happiness or sadness.

The process of stilling the mind starts with the knowledge that these emotional thoughts exist, this is acceptance. Then acknowledge that this is part of the process. Finally, be gracious to yourself. Acknowledge, accept, and be gracious. Since our emotions and feelings occur in degrees, we now know removing them will occur likewise in degrees or levels. By replacing these emotional feelings with an object, such as a lit candle, will help to diminish the dominance of your emotions during meditation. A longstanding and time-honored practice that helps, is focusing on the third eye, with eyes closed while chanting. As you practice these things, your thoughts will cease, at least as long as you continue with the practice. As you stop the thought chatter you will experience a degree of tranquility. That may last a view minutes or a longer period of time.

Your strong emotional feelings will diminish by degrees as long as you continue including meditation in a daily routine. There are degrees of emotions we bring to our meditation, depending on the time we've spent in silence and the state of mind we're in. While in meditation, we can evaluate our state of mind and see where we are concerning our emotional state.

After years of meditating, I found what works for me is to meditate with a chant, which helps to quiet my mind instantly as well as elevating my emotional state to the level of serenity and that always stills my mind.

SURRENDER BY BREATHING

One of the most beneficial acts in your spiritual journey is breathing. When an issue arises, instantly begin a cycle of conscious breathing. By stepping back mentally, while not letting emotions control the moment, surrender by closing your eyes, listening to the breath, which now becomes the only focus. Breath affects the mind, as well as the body and calms it down. This practice will become second nature. Keep on breathing until a reasonable feeling of calmness is achieved, within the heart and mind. Breath is the one thing we can control until it becomes an automatic response, then we just do it.

SURRENDERING THE EGO

One of the more enlightening experiences I mentioned in this book, was the admonition of Guru Gobind Singh for me to be patient. He also said I should be observant. To surrender our ego means putting our patience and our observations to the highest testing of our resolve.

When I reflected on what he told me I was moved to understand the context of what he said. I could not make a personal assumption of what he meant, because if I did that, I would be measuring his words by my own personal experiences of life. To truly and faithfully understand Guruji, I had to surrender my ego. For many of us who are on the path to spiritual enlightenment it is the supreme test of our commitment to truth and authenticity.

Ego stirs up old feelings from the past, while mixing it up with the present situation, thinking it must protect us now, and instantly takes control of the body as well as the mind. We know this by now, and this becomes an old story. Except, this is when we must surrender on a deeper level, one more time.

The two words that stood out from Guruji's counsel were "patience" and "observation." Both words implicitly denote a position of surrender. It also calls for an explicit expression by which we actively practice patience and observation. In essence this is precisely what we do when we practice meditation.

CHAPTER 11

"L.O.V.E" IS THE WAKE-UP CALL

When I sat at the Gurdwara for weeks and months, the things I felt were love, acceptance, belonging and serenity. Sitting in the presence of Guru, I felt I had come home.

With the practice of breathing, we become stronger. Mindfulness becomes our second nature and is directed purely at the self. Awareness as such needs to be directed at the self out of pure selfishness in order to find the true self within. Selfishness in this context is a means by which we absolutely direct all of our cognitive efforts towards a spiritual application of our very being in which our motives and intentions are involved.

I CALL THIS THE "L.O.V.E" MOMENT.

Leave everything, stop.
Observe your body.
Verbally ask: "What is going on, go deeper inward, start breathing deeply.
Exhale, recognize that you've maintained "LOVE FOR THE SELF."

TRANSFORMATION COMES ULTIMATELY

As we mature and wake up to our true nature, a transformation is occurring. In a sense we are liberated from our ego-driven nature; a calmness encompasses our whole being-ness. The outside world connects with the inner world on a richer level. The racing mind becomes still, and now witnesses the world with clarity. We finally understand that our transformation changes our views of ego-driven attachments. They do not serve us anymore and are ready to be examined and released.

At this stage, when we're paying attention to the signals that the body sends during a stressful situation, this means we listen, not only to the physical body, but to our "higher guidance," which helps us to see the signs and pay attention to them.

At times when I did not see the signs and just ignored any signal, disaster unfolded in front of me. Eventually, it became clear to me there are times when it is best to get out of my own way.

The higher guidance was signaling to me: "Leave everything, stop."

At first, this seemed unbelievable, even unreasonable, but inside I knew this was an intuition, a message I had to follow. It took courage to let myself surrender, telling ego it needed to go away.

After I stopped racing my mind, I practiced the next step, which is "Observe the body."

I pay attention to everything that my body does. In that moment I feel my heartbeat, I might feel anxious, I also listen to my breath. Is there any tension in the body and what can I do about it in this moment to relieve it?

To answer the question, I verbally ask: "What is going on?" I go deeper within, start breathing thoughtfully, as I scan my body. There is no judgment, just observation.

Through mindful awareness I surrender and give my burden over to a higher intelligence. It comes down to totally letting go of every belief, idea, and a set of behaviors from the past. Besides, what else could I lose? The initial experience of totally surrendering, letting go and letting God do the work, was during an intense hour of meditation. There, the feeling of trust I gained within myself was extraordinary, life was good. Looking back, I had complete charge of my life. It was like a movie playing, I'm taking part in a story without having any attachments and staying neutral. The meditations during those times were getting more focused.

This is when I implement "Exhale," recognize that you've maintained love for the self."

It was in one of those profound meditations in which I lost all awareness, judgments ceased. The mind felt weightless, the physical body lost its importance. The senses stopped searching on the inside, waiting for something to happen. I vanished in stillness, which I had not done before to this extent. Then beautifully quiet, a persistent, silent existence, not even observation. My mind was in a state of complete presence, yet the body was not going anywhere; it was distinctly different, yet it was the same. One thing became evident, the physical body is only the vehicle in the search for spirituality. The mind plays a huge role, and it recognized something. There is an observer of the observed. I felt a "presence." After coming out of meditation, I noticed a difference in my awareness; within the deep space of nothingness, there was an energy of observation present. What did it mean?

Recently, I was at the temple spending a silent moment, while I reflected on the "Naam." "Naam," according to devotees of the Sikh religion is the word of God and also means the essence of God. It is manifested by a ringing in the ears and can be accompanied by the sounds of celestial music. Devotees are able to acquire the sound through years of meditational practice.

Once you acquire the sound, it's like riding a bicycle, you never forget. After the Kundalini experience, I experienced the effects of what I now realize is "Naam." When it first occurred, I felt as if my hearing was internalized and that with every heartbeat, every breath, every movement of oxygen coursing through my body, created an audible sensation that I knew I had never experienced before and I didn't know what I felt, or what it meant. At first, I called it the sound of the Universe, because I didn't know what else to call it.

In the temple, as I meditated and reflected on how this affected my life, it became clear to me I wasn't the only person in the world who was affected by this phenomenon. In fact, I never felt it was a special thing to have this awareness. Since then, I simply accepted this has become part of my being-ness. What makes this important to me and the reason I write about this experience, is because the "Naam" has been with me for over thirty years and never left.

In the span of thirty years, after traveling in many countries, taught classes there, meditated consistently, and seemingly without knowing the reasons why I ended up in the Gurdwara in my hometown in Northern California, where I finally found out what I was hearing. Now I know I was led to this place, to this Temple, at this time in my life.

The Kundalini experience years ago was a force that, like an unstoppable flood opened channels of comprehension, leading from one awareness to another, finally leading me to illuminate the place that love occupies within a person's progression of spiritual growth. Love is the absolute connection to one's spiritual development. I have personally used love and the definitively practical acronym (L.O.V.E.) to further my own spiritual progress as a means to enhance my meditation practice. And in so doing reached the state of hearing "Naam," meaning to hear God's word.

WITH PRACTICE EVERYTHING BECOMES EASIER

At first there was no way I could feel love for myself, I never learned how. In my thirties I encountered the idea that one could not give love unless one had love to give in the first place. This was of great significance, which resulted in my being comfortable when I looked in the mirror and said, "I love you, I love you, I love you."

Eventually, I experienced self-love with total abandon. It simply happened. Finally, it dawned on me: I cannot share what I do not have, I can only share what is mine to give. As a wise person put it, love cannot be given away, it can only be shared. With daily practice I was able to overcome the lack of love for myself and eventually it became easier for me to see a bigger picture, of how love and self-acceptance go hand in hand.

PAY ATTENTION TO THE "SELF" WITH LOVE. THEN GO OUT WITH LOVE, PAY ATTENTION TO THE "OTHER"

When we're able to love ourselves, we're able to love everyone else too. Self-love touches everything within the body. Physical, mental and emotional. Love radiates like an ever-expanding energy; the vibration invites us to expand our heart, which helps to extend our vision. When we love ourselves, we trust ourselves. By extension, we can trust the world. We always make the right choices. Even if it turns out that one choice was not the best, it seemed the best at that moment. However, when we reflect on the historical or long view of one's choices, informed with the conscious application of love, the outcome always seems to result in beneficial ways.

As we move forward on our path to greater spiritual insight, we cultivate tenderness. Self-love is a powerful mechanism, that when

engaged there is no stopping it, for it brings joy and satisfaction. It is the circle that keeps on widening.

EGO SURRENDERS WHEN LOVE EXPANDS

It is time to sit and ask the questions.

"Does ego want to hurt me? No, it protects me!"

"Does ego rule me? No, it protects me!"

"Do I need ego to be in charge? No!"

"Do I love ego as part of me, quietly watching me? Yes, I love my ego."

CHAPTER 12

THE IMPACT
OF LOVE

My work sometimes can be rather stressful. In order to calm my agitated mind, I go to the temple daily, and sit with Guruji and listen if there is any wisdom that he can share with me. This is what I observed one day: I was particularly out of sorts and began to meditate. As soon as I sat for a couple of minutes this is the wisdom that came to me: Most things that create ego driven stress in your life are of your own doing. The negative issues from the past cannot harm you at the present time.

If ego needs to respond, for whatever reason, there can be no judgment just observation. I recognize that when in doubt, I give my ego a moment to act and watch intently where feelings progress to next. As ego wants to jump, and rectify an issue, in the next moment I present ego with love, and that makes it neutral instantly; beyond this idea, it helps that I recognize that deeply held beliefs I might still carry in the mind may also affect the way I handle my thoughts in this very moment.

As I become more and more skilled in letting go of how outside issues affect me, I become the great observer of how and when ego wants to protect me, I know with surety that I have no more fear of ego and how I will react, my mind is being deconditioned and this thing called ego is really all about awareness and grace, that I feel inside.

LOOKING BACK

As I come to my better senses, sitting in meditation, I realize how grateful I am to Guru Gobind Singh, sitting with me and holding my hand. As I observe the wider community, it would be reasonable for me to say that we all need someone to hold our hand. Our lives are informed by stressors that often create illusions of emptiness, depression, and the inability to solve our personal demons.

Our body is affected to such a degree, as to cause our nervous system to break down. Our effort to rebuild a broken-down mental state is often limited because there is a lack in our culture to acknowledge that the mind is more sensitive than we care to admit. Every single individual I have ever known in my life, has had some symptoms of mental depression.

It is absolutely possible to alter one's nervous system consciously, as I have witnessed for myself. For years I was extremely nervous, not knowing why; and when I had the Kundalini experience and the post effects related to the stresses in my body, it created a greater problem for my nervous system. I can candidly say that my life was improved, when I began to understand that my physical manifestations of a broken-down nervous system was in direct proportion to my spiritual growth.

In my personal experience with meditation, we can accomplish a calm outlook with focused breathing, which helps to slow us down. With our awareness directed inward, while identifying which triggers come from the outside, we can stop the negative emotions from entering this field that we call the body. When we recognize these stressors, we can decide how to handle them. The focus is inward, visualizing a calm, relaxed mind, now the body might be more open to receiving our inner signals that can help in a real way to quiet the nervousness, or anxiety. Soon the body will become very adaptable to positive change, responding to stress constructively. It is easy to learn this type of behavior. As always, there is a learning curve, however when committed to change and to awareness, the practice becomes fun.

Some years ago, my good friend's husband (they live in Northern Europe) developed a tumor on the brain. He had been hiking with his wife, up high in the Alps, when he collapsed. He had to be taken down the mountain by rescuers, and with a helicopter flown to the hospital.

The dark spot inside his brain was the size of a pea and in an area that would be hard to operate. Of course, doctors did everything they could, but left him with a few options. Eventually, the decision came down to surgically remove the tumor, despite knowing it was in a vulnerable area in the brain, which meant a positive outcome was not assured. My friends decided to try a healer who lived in their town and I offered to help with distance healing, here from Northern California.

The sessions from my house took place every day at a predetermined time. My friend with the tumor and I agreed, we would both focus at the same time of day for a healthy brain, asking God for a total healing and recovery. He had lost some functions in his body and was not stable when he walked. Within a few short weeks of engaging a healer in his native country and with my consistent effort sending him healing energy and praying for him, the tumor disappeared. When a follow-up scan was taken at the hospital, all that remained at that point was a dark spot the size of a pinhead. Later that disappeared too. He was totally tumor-free.

When he went to his doctor's appointment at a large university clinic, they were astonished. He was asked what he did to facilitate

the disappearance of the tumor, he explained what he had done. They encouraged him to continue and declared the disappearance of this clearly seen black spot on his brain, as a miracle.

Love generates an energy within the body that inhabits every single cell. As we awaken to this energy, its expression is expansive and grows exponentially breaking down all barriers and boundaries. The power of love is transformative, and it endures a lifetime.

CHAPTER 13

SEEING THE BIGGER PICTURE, PAST AND PRESENT

Now, years later it became apparent why all the clutter in my life had to be eliminated. The "Tenth Gate" opening stirred up deep-seated issues pushing everything to the surface. Anger had to be gotten rid of first, which I had plenty to work on. Next came walking in other people's shoes. Which was my way of learning empathy, feeling as if the pain is mine. Empathy is feeling with someone, walking or being in their sorrow. Empathy is not as much about the other person, as it is about oneself. It's really hard to express when the person you're interacting with is a mean person. It's always easy to show empathy to a little child who is weak and vulnerable. On the other hand, it's a challenge to express empathy to those who present negative personalities and hateful behaviors, such as racists, mean-spiritedness, and other traits that are antithetical to love.

RECOGNIZING VICTIMHOOD

Having to wake up from victimhood myself, empathy, or walking in someone's shoes, helped me significantly to awaken to the victim I could become so easily. The "Tenth Gate" opening was involuntary and the most glorious but also the most painful experience of a lifetime. Especially soon after the ecstasy wore off, I was the victim. Many lessons came along. Back then I could not see them. Self-imposed darkness was my companion for many years. Yet, I had the light inside me all along.

It was because of the darkness that I eventually decided enough was enough. I had to get angry, fed up with the world and myself, before any changes could take place. It was my experience of victim as a child, which I needed to remember. I needed to honor my feelings and cry out loud.

A dear friend, who listened to me, helped me to resolve the anger. She asked me very skillfully what I really wanted. I was telling her exactly what I wanted to satisfy the hurt child within me. I needed to humiliate the people who humiliated me. Just expressing what I had not expressed, opened my heart and letting anger hang out.

The anger energy generated in that moment, which I held for years, pushed the victim right out of me. It helped to resolve my anger. Within minutes, I started to see light ahead, without darkness looming over me. What helped? Expressing anger honestly, without feeling guilty, while creating boundaries for myself. When anger pipes up now, it's not deep anger, just irritation and I can say: "Hey I don't like this." I've created a space where I feel safe and express what I don't like. This was simply impossible for me before this moment, I released years of surpressed anger.

DISCOVERING MORE GIFTS

The "Tenth Gate" when opened, removes the blocks. Which means developing awareness, observing thoughts and actions, which initially was serious work for me. I can spot ego a mile away, my own and other's. I experience many moments of levity by laughing and living in the moment, like a child, I was meant to be. Living freely, with innocence and joy. I appreciate that the silence within is not silence at all, but wisdom waiting to be expressed.

Speaking your truth is encouraged. Look at your truth, discuss it if needed without judgment, acknowledge it and move forward. Whatever our experiences may be, if there is an emotional value attached to your truth, while not clearly seen, perceptions may be tainted. If there is attachment, we must neutralize the emotions. Let there be no mistake, emotions have to be examined and felt to the strongest intensity that one can muster; sit with that intensity as long as there is need, once that is accomplished, we are able to let them go. Many spiritual seekers I have met are in the process of having to unblock the old emotional pattern, before there can be a progression into deeper consciousness.

Whether one had the "Tenth Gate" opened or not, the spiritual evolution is well under way, and we are seeking to let go of old patterns which have kept us captive emotionally. Striving to release old patterns of behavior or beliefs which do not serve us any longer, is a huge step towards awakening. The path becomes one of pure devotion. Becoming authentic to the self. Letting the Universe, God, reign. Trusting that all guidance comes from the higher power. At the same time recognizing the power within and the direction we choose is our birthright. Then joy comes back, and fear leaves for good. Only now I am beginning to see what the benefits of my long, arduous journey are.

The gifts of meditation turn life into tranquility, even when chaos reigns outside. We observe serenity within as we're vibrating with good energy. The body is able to disperse this energy to all connections, especially those who are aware and want to receive it. The dysfunctions of my previous life are mostly gone. As a matter of fact, when I see dysfunction coming towards me, I look at it, smile and let it go right past me. When friends tell me their story of dysfunction, I listen but also let it pass. Unless they ask for advice, there is no need to rescue. These days, it's easy to spot unresolved issues and their causes.

When I observe my fellow travelers, I understand the path that they're on, since I would like to believe I'm on the same journey. We can share our wisdom, if we are asked and want to be heard. Not every traveler is open or understands.

My initial and simple advice when asked, is to meditate, including concentrated breathing. That is my remedy for everything. Breathe and let go, have no attachments to any outcome, just acceptance. On the other hand, be open with empathy to share your wisdom without judgment when advising sincere fellow travelers or others on the same path to spiritual growth.

GURUJI

These days I see Guruji as a blue color spot. Other times I watch him in my mind's eye. He is clearly in front of me. Just a couple of days ago I was sitting and watching people bowing down at the altar inside the Gurdwara. A young woman had her baby with her and laid him down on his tummy, his head touching the carpeted floor. Guruji was there right above them. He smiled and his love radiated within the prayer hall. What a beautiful sight to behold.

A few days later, I was sitting at the prayer hall. I said a prayer, then spoke to Guruji:

"I have not seen you today and would like to see you."

In the very next moment, blue sprinkles that looked like real water appeared in midair, just like a fountain. The water disappeared before it touched the ground. It showered for a little while as I sat and watched. What a delight, I thanked Guruji.

Again a few days later, I went to the Gurdwara to meditate. Lately, I have been listening to a certain song, that's played when there are no prayers. I entered the prayer hall and asked Guruji if I could hear my favorite Kirtan, (spiritual music). The pleasure was all mine. The public address system in the temple started playing that song instantly! It was glorious. I thanked Guruji.

Just as quickly as the music started, it was over. I asked Guruji: "What happened to the music?"

The answer came right back: "He did not listen."

"Oh," I said: "That makes sense."

The Granthi who just happened to turn on the music was not paying attention to Guruji's wishes. He had played another song. I was in a dilemma. My thought was this:

"Should I tell him that Guruji was talking to him?"

I wanted to think about this and went to the Langer Hall and ate some food. Then decided to ask Guruji to send someone who could translate because the Granthi does not speak English well enough to understand what I was about to tell him. I went back inside for meditation. It was not too long before a woman walked in and sat close to me. Sitting there I contemplated what to do. By then the Granthi, who also had lunch came inside, I approached him, by walking up to him and said:

"Why did you not turn the music back to the "Wahe Guru" song?"

He did not understand me and went to the woman who sat close to me and asked if she could translate. The lady translated it to the Granthi, and he then proceeded to play the "Wahe Guru" song.

He came back and sat down, then I related the information back to him. I thought about the fact that Guruji's words were lost on him, but he was not able to hear or listen. The Granthi asked the translating woman to ask me:

"Did you say that Guru Gobind Singh was speaking to me?"

"Yes, he was, but you did not listen."

With a broad smile, he looked around and said: "You can see Guru Gobind Singh?"

"Yes, I see him, and hear him."

Again, he smiled and said something in Punjabi. The lady translator said: "You are lucky, not many people get to have this kind of a thing happen to them."

"Yes, I understand."

All of us chatted for a bit, while another Granthi joined us. It was a pleasant exchange.

When we were alone the lady translator confided, "I was on my way home when I had this strong urge to come to the Gurdwara. It's not close to my house, and the drive is out of my way. This great urge took over me, I had to come to the Gurdwara."

When the lady arrived at the Gurdwara the Granthi asked if she could translate what I had said. "You had asked that someone who speaks English should come and translate. Guess what? I'm from England. How much better can it get?" She added.

"Yes, that is true," I said.

The woman and I were chatting for probably two hours, exchanging ideas and telling stories. We both believe in the mysterious ways of the Universe, and how we can be directed in the exact manner that help us and others in very unexpected ways. The secret is we must be specific and ask precisely for what we want.

CHAPTER 14

"KUNDALINI RISING" OR THE "TENTH GATE" OPENING

More than thirty years ago, I had an incredible experience. At the time I was not sure what it was. I had heard of this thing called Kundalini. It is an energy residing within the body. In the Eastern traditions it's called Kundalini or the "coiled snake," which rests in the lowest part of the spine. The Sikhs call it the "Tenth Gate," after the energy rises, and opens on the top of the head, the crown.

Every living human being has this mechanism, this sleeping energy, that can be awakened; it arises either spontaneously, or by serious devotional habits, meditation, and specific yogic practices including pranayama. (Specific ways of breathing)

Although this wisdom is thousands of years old, I have never heard a report on the radio about this energy or seen articles in any magazines written about it. Not many scientists or spiritual adepts have taken up the research on Kundalini.

Spirituality, or more precisely, super consciousness, is not something to be pushed away lightly. The "Tenth Gate" energy awakened is just the beginning for humanity to reach different levels of awareness. Why otherwise would this energy be inside of everyone? Once it is activated, a major energetic shift occurs.

The mind undertakes a reflective journey of awakening. The whole system undergoes a tremendous physical and energetic change, causing life-altering transformations.

Previous to the beginning of the opening of the "Tenth Gate" I heard an intense, loud buzzing sound that lasted for several days. My whole body felt as if a swarm of bees had taken up residence in my head. It was accompanied by a crawling feeling, up and down my spine.

The sensation felt like sexual arousal. The lower part of my body was in agitation. The feelings became stronger as if I needed to explode, up and out with every fiber in my body. Soon it became evident I had no choice over what was about to happen, or when it was going to happen. I was extremely restless for several more days.

At one point I hoped the energy would subside, but the force hit me like a tornado, over-taking my body. It was strongest in the lowest part of my torso, where I felt a storm brewing, gathering strength inside my belly. Then it intensified in the spine with a sound like that made by the rushing water of Niagara Falls. Right before the sendoff, I was helpless and in a panic. An incredible amount of energy built up in the bottom of my spine and was about to be unleashed. I closed my eyes and lost awareness for a moment. I felt like a powerful rocket lifting off its launch pad.

That night the energy rose up from the bottom of my spine to my shoulders, across my chest to the solar plexus, back to the shoulders, through the neck and finally to the top of my head. In a split second, my crown felt as if the lid was blown off. My chest was trembling. Within minutes the physical or more strenuous part was over. It seemed as if my body had burrowed through a tunnel and came out on the other side. The energy I felt inside was indescribable.

After the initial force settled, I became aware of infinite openness in the crown. The body felt as if it was surging with electricity. It was very pleasant yet natural as the energy moved throughout my body, up and down, mostly in the spine. The whole body was involved, but the spine is the lightning rod. I was hot and cold and in a state of rapture, which lasted from Sunday night until Tuesday at 1:00 PM when the ecstasy wore off. Inside my body was a light of such intensity that blinded me.

While in this state, I experienced a great expansiveness as if there were no differences between myself and any human being. The next day at work - I was working as a massage therapist at that time - my energy was either appealing to my clients, or it frightened them away. My fingers and hands massaged their skin, but I could not tell where my hands began, or where their skin ended. It was like we were one and the same entity.

Now nature took on a special glow, trees had an aura of white around them. But by far and the most interesting point was that I had acquired a deep understanding of the psyche as I interacted with other people, and their very being was like an open book, their life stories were revealed to me.

GAINING NEW ABILITIES

As the weeks and months passed, new experiences opened up for me, and I gained certain skills and abilities. For instance, my dreams were more vivid, but at the same time they were prophetic. The dreams portrayed future events, which at times scared me because I often never knew what was happening to whom, where, and when.

So I began to make notes of my dreams, and thought I'd better ask what the dream messages are and for whom they were meant. It turned out the dreams were premonitions. One day this strange idea came to me: Let me hear my dream results on the radio. This way I learned the names, location and specific events that occurred in my dreams and they were verified on the radio news. In my dreams the events had already taken place several days, weeks or months before they were aired on the radio. This caused a troubling dilemma for me because I could not contact anyone to let them know about the dreams and tell them of events that will occur in the future. Of major concern to me was that certain individuals involved in those dreams were people I knew very well. Some I knew only in passing. Others were total strangers.

Although I had prophetic dreams before the Kundalini opening, those dreams were location specific, whereas now my dreams entailed a wider global scale that reached out to all humanity on earth. It was as though I could now understand the very psychic nature of this planet we call Earth.

Again, here I felt I did not want to know about other people crashing their airplane. Or being in a car accident. At one point it was enough, I asked not to get this kind of dream or insights again. And with that request the dreams stopped. The burden to know how other people's life can or will progress, was profoundly disturbing to me. I wished not to know. And asked with kindness to be taken away from such knowledge.

Although the Kundalini experience brought an overpowering awareness to me, it also presented a lot of uncertainty. At that time, I was not able to handle this energy with insight and with the fullest wisdom possible.

About a year later I noticed a shift of the nutritional needs of my body. To mitigate the problem, I needed more energy foods because my metabolism increased. The food modifications (I liked potatoes, cooked carrots, lots of butter and bread, all root vegetables, plenty of legumes, brown rice, etc.) made a noticeable change in my physical health.

Also, my hearing became sensitive to loud music on the radio, that I had to close my ears. I also developed an extraordinary sight and can see things that are inaccessible or invisible to most people. Spirit energies or circles of energy with playful lights swirled in the air. Clear globes filled with electrical currents and different colors appeared out of nowhere. Orbs that hover above people, sometimes over furniture or rooms were constantly visible.

One day I told a friend of mine that I could take a fork and bend it. My friend had seen me accomplish some unusual things before. He was up for more stuff that would just amuse him. I took a fork out of the drawer and held the handle below the tines with my forefinger and thumb. Then I gently moved them back and forth. I took several deep breaths and lo and behold, the fork bent right between my fingers. My friend asked if he could try it. Of course, I was all for it. He took several deep breaths, concentrated really hard – to no avail, the fork didn't move. He still brings this phenomenon up sometimes in conversations.

Often, I could see a person's life play out like a movie, when the person entered my space at work. In the beginning, it was all interesting. But it got old very fast. There are as many tragedies as there are people and I was not spared with visions for my own family. Many times, sadness overtook me. Eventually, I asked God to be relieved of this insight.

To make things worse, I went crazy looking for the rapture and would give anything to feel bliss again, but it was not going to happen. Ecstasy was nowhere to be found. Several months had passed, my emotional state became bleak, sometimes melancholic. Acute tiredness set in; my circuits had been blown. My mind was filled with air and a hum.

SOLACE

The only thing that brought solace was when I closed my eyes and I was engulfed with light. It still surrounds me now, no matter what happens. The white light takes over when I close my eyes, the mind disappears in that moment and nothing exists.

Daily meditation takes me to the place where I meet God. Bliss envelops me in the midst of the Universe. The visions are mystical. It is not the exact kind of ecstasy as the very first time. However, it feels comforting, and this paradise is just a breath away.

In this mystical place, I see Guru Gobind Singh in all his glory. He is right next to me on my left shoulder. I feel his presence. Most days he shows up when I'm at the Gurdwara. He literally appears in form. Not in human form, but blue in the shape of a rectangle, although the size changes often.

CHAPTER 15

THE BODY IS THE TEMPLE

After the Kundalini experience, I recognized I needed to take care of my physical body even more than before; I always understood that I had to take care of my body. I was a vegan for some time but went to vegetarianism. That suited my needs better.

I attended classes and received a certificate to become a "Resistance Stretching" facilitator. I had to be in harmony with my body. To do so I had to implement strict rules for myself. The affect of the Kundalini energy changed my body drastically. My mind and body had to be aligned, I felt as if there was a disconnect between both. It felt like I was at a train terminal running and trying to board an already moving train.

Although I was an herbalist and a holistic practitioner, I knew enough to understand the dynamics of a healthy body and what necessitates it. The Kundalini force altered everything I knew about health and a balanced system. The strong influence gave me a sense that I was not only out of kilter in my mind and body, but my soul was lacking too. My holistic training and up-bringing taught me that we, as sentient beings need balance in order to function in the highest possible capacity. To achieve my personal constitutional needs, I became aware of my nutritional needs very early in life, and to the present day I'm still a vegetarian. One of the delights in attending the temple is the vegetarian food served daily, which is one of the tenets of the Sikh religion.

THE PRACTICE OF SLOWING DOWN AND NOTICING

The body carries a heavy load, especially if there is a lot of stress generated in the mind. What beliefs fuel the anxiety in the mind is of great consequence to our health. The change starts from inside to the outside by paying attention to two things at the same time: feeling what is transpiring, both physically and emotionally.

This is a practice and may take a while. We learn to pay attention to the self with a remarkable discipline. The following exercise will help in creating certain fundamental changes in your life.

Please read this section before starting. We go into the process by slowing down the breath. This is nostril breathing. The focused, single-minded approach begins with inhaling and counting to five. Then exhaling, counting to ten. If at first, this is too strenuous, count to three then exhale to six.

Establish a set amount of breaths until it becomes natural. Soon increase the number of breaths until this also becomes comfortable. The exercise might take a week or two of daily practice and if you're slow with the breathing exercises, the full exercise cycle may take a full month to become established. This is perfectly fine, please practice daily.

The next step is to breathe in, count to five; hold breath, count to five; exhale to the count of ten, (double the number).

It looks like this: Breathing in, while counting to five. Holding, while counting to five. Exhaling, counting to ten.

Eventually the "holding breath" is the same length as the "exhalation." The space between the breaths is where we begin to feel "stillness." You are now developing a breathing system, while discovering the silence between each breath.

The breathing might only last two to five minutes. It is the jumping board of recognizing and witnessing for yourself how it feels to be quiet, to focus the mind.

As we get better in our practice, we become aware of other nuances within the body by continuing the fundamentals of breathing. Is the body agitated before starting the breathing? Is the breath quiet or hurried? Is the body responding to the breath by slowing down or speeding up? These nuances will become important, as we want to slow down our stressed-out body or slow down an out of control blood pressure and thus release a migraine headache or improving overall health and immunity. These are many benefits of breathing with awareness. We can change the body chemistry and become mindful by using breathing as a tool for health.

CONTROLLING BREATH, CONTROLLING LIFE

To balance out the body we must look at how breath affects the body. How it controls life and larger aspects of daily functioning. We use breath as the vehicle for letting go of thoughts and surrendering ego; it provides us the personal as well the internal guidance to move forward in many ways.

Because of its simplicity we may not see the beneficial influences at first, but with time and self-observation, we can distinguish how breathing directly affects our spiritual equilibrium and improves our emotional state.

Breath, when practiced to its fullest extent is the most powerful teacher in relation to mindfulness. With mindfulness, we are not victim to the body or mind, and eventually we become less and less influenced by the roller-coaster ride of our emotions.

Instead, they become waves, which rise slightly and recede easily, nothing drastic and are immediately released. There are no more resentments to hold unto. We become skillful with conscious breathing, influencing the physical and spiritual aspect of who we are, which ultimately leads us to a path of an unassuming easygoing style of receiving the world.

More importantly, it succeeds in bringing us closer to an awareness of a more expansive sense of self. Breath is the bridge from actual physical experience to the ethereal interconnectedness with all living things. As we're breathing, life moves along. As we consciously breathe, life becomes awareness.

CHAPTER 16

WE HAVE SURRENDERED ON A DEEPER LEVEL

We love our self, and experience unity within. Connection to the self without reservation is connection to God. This is instinctual, it is felt as a warm and fuzzy feeling. There is no way to explain this otherwise.

Ego does not rule us or believes it needs to protect us. We value peace of mind as a state of being-ness; we feel love for the whole of humanity. Humility appears, which transports us into a state of awe and wonder; while grace becomes our steady companion. We have gone through what is explained in Anand (u) Sahib in the summary of teachings

"The Sacred Nitnem"

1. *Union with God confers to supreme bliss.*

We have given up control, have surrendered. We experience the abundance of love and bliss and recognize the power of God. (Author's note)

2. *The Sermon to the mortal and his soul.*

When we attach the mind to our Higher Power and love God, we can throw our fears away forever.

When we trust the Self, we trust God; the higher power is our safety net. Trust becomes the cement of the soul. It holds us together, brings confidence. Fear has lost its power of influence. Ego has lost its authority. (Author's note)

(vii) *Mortal's eyes will see God in everyone and at every place.*

When the true Guru showers his grace, man sees the reality and finds that the world is the manifestation of God. He finds God present within himself, at every place and in everyone. No one is evil. He sees God has put his light in their eyes so that he may see truth and reality.

When we experience God's love, our eyes and heart have to be open and in silence, listening to the voice within. We are in communion and contemplation. Fear cannot exist in this realm. God displays his true divinity because we have surrendered, given up control.

We see natural forces gracefully flowing by design. Wishes are granted through intention. We see the divine energy of God through the eyes of humility. Accepting that God is present in all and showers gifts to all who are present with God. Seeing good in all, creating the world as God intended; free from ill will and unrestricted, to choose what the soul wishes to see. These are the gifts bestowed upon those who are awakened and touched by God. Being present with God takes an open heart and spirit. It is our birthright. (Author's note)

3. *The Divine Orchestral Music.*

As God manifests himself in the devotee's mind, he sees the divine light within himself. He observes in others the divine light. God grants the divine music to be heard. A true happiness fills the heart. His soul merges into the supreme soul, even as he remains in this world.

Divine music is the sound that makes the heart swell with happiness. It is the sound of the celestial orchestra, that starts with the stroke of a bell, and other heavenly instruments. Any sound we hear from within, is the "unstruck" sound, God's music that is playing for the mortal's ears to hear.

Another sound is the constant humming of the Universe, that I hear every moment of the day. It's like the current in the river with perpetual movement flowing steadily to the ocean. The sounds are genuine and there is no rational explanation for it. It is humanity's connection to God's timelessness. (Author's note)

Other things are also happening. Visions of electrical energies appear as bright colors, apparitions of human figures become visible. The Universe appears on the screen of the mind. The force of the unseen Universe is recognized.

THE TRUE SAINT DEFINED

They travel on the most difficult and peculiar path. They throw away their pride and seek their God-given desires.

When we make the conscious choice to walk the path with God, it is not an easy endeavor. It is not an easy road to travel. We must recognize that we live in a world where judgments reign, while we learn to put aside our ego, and admittedly these realities in life are not easy to negotiate. Yet, we know the path is open and the one that helps us, is God. As we walk the walk with humility, we surrender with love on a deeper level. (Authors note)

CHAPTER 17

DEEPER INSIGHTS STILL RECOVERING

It was a sunny day, when I sat in meditation inside the temple. My day was slow at work and I had plenty of time to sit with Guruji. Before getting started I spent outside in the courtyard in the sun. It was warm that summer. I had examined the flowers growing in the beds. The pink and red roses reminded me of the times when I lived in Europe as a little girl and memories welled up.

I'm in the temple now still wondering how my life has gone from my European roots to a deep appreciation of a different and sometimes surprising cultural shift. And yet, I have a deep respect for all the people I have come to know. I feel a sense of security sitting here, but there was a moment in my life when I did not have this feeling.

Inexplicably I felt his presence, Guruji entered my thoughts. I felt enveloped with the protection of his love. My mind still wandered and suddenly as if hit by a sour note, I began to feel very sad. Tears flowed down my cheeks, and momentarily I was embarrassed. People were looking at me, I had to get up and get a napkin for my tears.

As I reflected my sadness grew and I realized I had to sit and examine why this sadness was so overwhelming. Upon reflection, it occurred to me, my sadness was the result of the loss of a sibling relationship, which resulted in several years of not speaking with each other up to now. It felt as if I lost a very dear friend. These emotional wounds just took me to a place that overwhelmed my senses and tears flowed freely. Not out of regret or retribution, but rather of release. Sadness, accompanied by doubt and loss, were expressed with the tears in the temple. I felt Guruji's presence before me as he encouraged me to surrender the overwhelming emotion.

When we finally decide to walk on the path of spirituality, we wake up the process of seeing different perceptions of how life can run easily and quietly, simply and sweetly, but also at times with heartbreaking sadness. Did you get what you wanted, or as you planned? You eventually recognize that life always has a way coming around. In hindsight, sometimes things worked out better than expected. Why is that? Because we stepped back and let life take its own road, because in those moments of confusion and selfdoubt we surrendered.

LIVING IN THIS MOMENT

MEDITATION BECOMES A STATE OF "BEING-NESS"

That's the idea of meditation. There are no secrets, no special ways of getting into a state of enlightenment. What it takes is a commitment to be in the space of silence and learn to focus. Practice it every day and use as many tools as are available. Study meditation with someone who knows from direct experience, and who is committed to your growth and gives encouragement.

By sticking to your commitment, you will enter a place of magnificence. The mind has finally learned to focus, the thinking part has relented. An outer-worldly experience is finally coming to meet you.

The moment you allow your mind to focus, stillness becomes part of your world. Sitting in silence deepens the calmness within. The quietness becomes a source of joy, while peace befalls your inner landscape. The way you experience your life is changing even more.

When you observe how your daily meditation affects you, another deeper understanding becomes evident, there is no difference between you and everything that you see. Moreover, everything you do, feel or think influences someone. Everything someone touches affects you too. And in the next second, an even greater realization hits; you're in a state of pure consciousness, pure joy, surrounded by pure essence. Knowing that contentment dwells within your soul, and the entirety of your world is present deep within. Do you understand what that means?

The ether in the Universe is one big ocean, you are the drop of water in that ocean, you are part of the energy that connects everything to all things. You are pure energy. In one spark of a moment time stands still. Awareness is delicate in this space; abilities might come to an immediate forefront for you to recognize. Time is of no consequence, and the Universe is yours, dive in deep.

CHAPTER 18

WHEN EGO DISAPPEARS

The world may look different after an extraordinarily deep meditation. The gradual waking up to the change appears as if the world has offered up its slower pace to us. The scenery within is utterly rearranged.

The inability to change from preconceived ideas of how life is or should be are mostly gone. The last hardcore beliefs are still changing and evolving. Emotions and ego are not entangled anymore. Dislikes to long-held ideas are turning into acceptance; willingness to see life with the eyes of neutrality makes judgements disappear.

MEETING THE RIGHT TEACHER

On the road to spirituality some people are teachers and they become our guides. They are respected but never worshipped. The guidance from teachers is just that, guidance. When we meet such a person, let the heart speak and feel if this is the right guide for you.

A teacher must have firsthand experience with deep meditation, and intuitively allow us to be who we are and point us toward our individual journey. The path must be chosen by the individual and can never be achieved by force.

When the seeker is ready to make a commitment, there will be an affirmative response from one's inner voice. As the student, we make the best effort. Since the path is experiential in all aspects of our being, emotions are involved. This is natural, for it also invites ego to express opinion. We watch the quality of emotions we bring to our lesson and learn to discern, we express what we feel and resolve the issue without letting ego take over.

A true fellow seeker and guide will ask: "What do you think?" This guidance gives encouragement, and lets you find your way.

Some truths may be uncomfortable to look at. Your guide will find a way to reach your heart by the simplest means. Sometimes the guide will have to firmly nudge you to explore uneasy things. And that is the reason for a guide or teacher to be available.

There may be moments when we are still blinded by our shortcomings. A teacher can help to sort issues out, with honesty and kindness. We must be willing to listen and at the same time put ego aside.

WHAT HAPPENS WHEN
WE LOVE EGO?

Ego is the obstacle that is like the big boulder that gets in the way of life. One way we can recognize ego as the big wall that we erect around us, is when we experience lack. Let's look closer and understand that ego is only there to protect. But now we go a step beyond of what might be expected.

We go and search out ego to love it unconditionally. What that really means for me personally, when I get into a situation and ego needs to pipe up, I recognize an uneasy feeling in my gut, my solar plexus. That's where ego sits for me. That's also where I feel ego piping up. When there is an uneasy feeling, anywhere inside my body, I pay close attention, so no feelings escape me, and I wonder where the lack originates.

The truth is, once we've learned to listen, there is no mistake. Our gut-level, when it speaks has a clear, recognizable language. It signals powerfully when something is off. No matter why ego rears its head, we love it. That means precisely, I stop what I'm doing, take a deep breath and recognize that it is me who needs reassurance, and more precisely love. After a couple of deep breaths, I'm back to my equilibrium and can go on with my next project.

It is always me who needs love in order for my ego to calm down. When my emotional needs are met, there is no wall of separation between ego and myself. It's always me who wanted love and understanding. Ego has no need to do anything, because the lack within ego has been addressed, because ego is me, embodied.

At the same time we are learning how to love our ego, this gives us the opportunity to look at humanity's ego with the same discerning non-judgmental love. Will this be easy? Not in the beginning, or maybe it will. All we do is to understand why a person is letting ego rule their mind or heart and give them the benefit of our compassion.

Recently I was at the Gurdwara. I sat on a spot that was flanked on both sides with cushioned stools. It was spacious enough for one person to sit comfortably with no restrictions. However, a lady wanted to sit right next to me. She asked me to move over. So, I did, not very willingly, I must add. Because the stools were on both sides of us, we were now in a very tight space. I felt squeezed in and I had to stretch out my legs and could not sit lotus style. This irritated me a bit. As I looked at her from the side, it dawned on me, I was being judgmental. That part of my thinking I wanted to change. I knew in that moment ego got the better of me. My countenance changed. As soon as I recognized ego, I changed towards her and surmised she must have had a good reason why she wanted to sit in this tight spot. Truthfully, I don't think she was very comfortable either. But we sat there for a long while, as I had my attitude adjustment, I decided to really love this situation, including her.

Inside my heart I felt at peace and looked at her with a smile, I don't know if she could tell the change in me. She suddenly asked if I had room. And of course, I did. Prayers were going on at the Gurdwara. Unexpectedly, she decided to get up and find another spot. There was plenty of room everywhere else. That moment showed me, when I change my attitude the circumstances also change. This was not the first time I reigned in my ego, and it disappeared. So did any judgment on my part. The wall inside me vanished within seconds.

There was nothing physical I had to do. My mind gained awareness, the heart changed, including my attitude. Ego acted up, I felt it. My heart opened and the attitude was lifted.

Often, when I experience a shift in my thinking, my perception changes, my outlook changes and so do my circumstances.

I will tell of a more insightful story. I experienced this a long time ago. This is powerful, in the sense that I wanted something, yet I had no attachment to it. My husband, his mom, her husband and myself went to a seminar. When we registered, we were told to sign up for the door prizes. When I saw what the door prizes were, I got very excited and declared that the first prize was mine. We filled out our tickets and placed them in a box.

Halfway through the seminar it was raffle time. I was very excited and told my mother-in-law that the first prize tape set was mine. The speaker was very inspirational, and now I wanted those tapes even more.

He placed his hand in the drum with all the tickets and called out the name Kevin. Quickly I stood up and said: "It's Karin."

My husband was embarrassed and pulled me down. I stood up again. The speaker on stage looked at me (I was in row one), and he read the ticket again. He said, "Oh yes, it's Karin." Of course, not my husband or anyone else could hold me back. I had to give my last name and then the speaker knew he had the right person.

Before he called my name, I knew those tapes were meant for me. It was as clear as daylight. But I did not have any attachment to the them.

Often, I knew what life had in store for me. There is a knowing that resides within all of us, we have to learn and listen to our inner voice, it will let us know what's coming. There is a feeling when I get a premonition. It's my gut level, I can't easily explain this, but there is a surety within me when I know something that hasn't happened yet, but it will soon. I could give my right arm and know that something specific will be happening. It begins with opening the mind to possibilities, letting it happen. Ego can never enter this playing field.

In my neighborhood lived a young woman. She lived upstairs from me. Every night when she came home, she made extraordinarily loud noises. This was always late at night. I tried talking to her and that made her really angry. Finally, I called the police. Several times while talking to the police they could not understand her behavior either. One late evening I overheard her say to the police officer: "I promise, I'll get better. I will have to overcome my pride."

Now what did that mean? Instantly, I recognized she was caught by ego. That helped me to realize and see the need to love her attitude. It seemed that's what needed loving. Very cautiously I began to send her love and compassion. Why cautiously? I can't say. It seemed the right thing at the time. Within a few days the noisy, wild child had calmed down. I barely knew she was there.

I began to think of her welfare, her soul. I sent her the energy of love. This was not easy at first, but it became easier with time, and soon I was determined to love this young woman, no matter what happened.

The wisdom I can take from this experience, when you don't know what to do, is to send the energy of love. In essence, I let go of my ego and loved hers.

CHAPTER 19

THE "TENTH GATE" OPENING EXAMINED AGAIN

The opening of the "Tenth Gate" is a life-changing event. I will do my best to explain the sensations and feelings that I felt inside, while both my mind and body were hurled towards an indescribable feeling of bliss.

Although I experienced feelings of depression after the opening of the "Tenth Gate," I realize now that those feelings of despair were deeply held repressed and unresolved emotions that needed to be extricated from my psyche. As such, the "Tenth Gate" provided a spiritual and psychological cleansing.

While the body is involuntarily engaged, its function is to be the portal towards ecstasy. The mind willingly, although hesitantly at first, collapses into the euphoria that unfolds inside. The physical form is the vehicle that moves us towards the opening of the "Tenth Gate." The brain still functions but has nothing to do except to be the witness of the experience. In this moment where total awareness arises, light literally pervades everything that exists in the internal and external world. Indescribable euphoria accompanies the light, growing involuntarily within the mind and body. The sensation is of absolute bliss and complete connection to everything.

Almost immediately a notably different awareness is felt. It seemed that I became an intrinsic part of the world, not just the world itself, but in the world, and I sensed that I was watching myself and I was witnessing my very being. The soul seemed to be growing outward, as a distinct kind of knowingness which enhanced this event. The Universe itself appeared to be wise. The sensitivity of the five senses increased with a staggering intensity.

A startling knowledge triggers your cognition, that this event is of a particularly different level, through which you absolutely know that the world seems to be aware, too. It has its own wisdom.

Moreover, other senses become noticeable, as they show up later. White lights like an intense aura begin to envelop all trees, rocks, animals, people, and everything in nature, and by an extension, even objects that are invisible to the human eye reveal themselves in wondrous ways.

I would hear heavenly noises coming from within like musical instruments playing beautiful and harmonious music, as well as humming noises as if an electrical current is continuously running through my head. A most remarkable experience was when I could audibly hear what people over very long distances away were saying.

As it turns out, the body only plays a small part in this rapture. To begin with, this energy exists within every human body. That means we all have the same chance to experience this incredible energy.

Eventually, something bigger takes over. While the feelings within the body are lifted into ecstasy, at some point one's physicality is itself left behind. One becomes the active observer within this spiritual experience. In this moment where everything is left behind, the intellect integrates with a deeper wisdom, and the only choice is to sweetly surrender.

Within the ether, no singularity of being-ness exists. The soul merges with the Supreme Soul. Everything seems alive at this moment, with no boundaries. Within minutes of witnessing the vastness of the Universe in front of my eyes, with lights streaming in, an infinite awareness befalls that part of me who is the observer. There is a presence. In a moment, I become the infinite, because I recognize the "infinite."

I (as in "myself") does not exist at this moment. The "I" of myself vanishes. Energy exists only as a collective, and at this moment the soul is recognized as the infinite.

In a split second of awareness, my perceived single soul space vanishes, but rises within a sea of souls, vastly expanding. Singularity does not exist. Everything exists at once. Where unconsciousness reigned, it is now transformed into pure conscious wisdom.

The space I am existing in now is the space where everything exists, past present and future. The immortal soul in its purest form is gathered here, to the fullest of its potentiality. No duality exists. Pure consciousness abides here. It is divine, undiluted, everlasting and incredibly bright.

CHAPTER 20

IS DAILY LIFE POSSIBLE BEYOND BLISS?

After experiencing ecstasy, I then experienced moments of doubt, and I agonized with the feeling that bliss may not be a constant companion. I wavered between pain and ecstasy. Sometimes when pain took over, the struggle became unbearable, which made the path difficult. I was lonely and desperate and had no teachers to answer my questions. I felt lost and confused in this physical world of finite energy.

This was my experience after the powerful energy wore off. It took several months to get back to my normal way of behaving and living. The person who was me up to that fateful moment is gone now. A different way of understanding life has established itself within my mind, body and soul.

Many years have passed since. I'm waking up to my life now. Amazingly, I survived and made a commitment to stay focused on my spiritual path. This road I've travelled was not easy, but I would not change it. The rewards are miraculous.

When I look at the life of Guru Gobind Singh, I recall the great suffering he and his family endured for their beliefs and the road they chose to travel towards enlightenment, and I am content to know that suffering is a universal experience in this life.

Seeing Guru Gobind Singh at the Temple has made my path the easier road travelled. Yet, I still have my moments.

TRUSTING IN THE MOMENT

In a moment of doubt, I asked Guruji: "Why am I coming here daily, to the Gurdwara. Is there a reason that I don't understand?"

The answer came in the form of a mental vision: Looking out in front of me was a field of wheat.

"What is a field of wheat showing me?" I asked Guruji.

"It looks like it needs to be harvested."

Instantly a second picture entered my mind. I see the word "patience" spelled out for me.

"Oh, this means the harvest is coming. I need to be patient!"

This is what happens as I wait for insights to come to me. The best advice I give myself is to stay in the present moment. That makes life easier. I focus on what's right in front of me, trusting that all is well.

WHAT IS MY NEW LIFE?

Daily activities have taken many interesting turns. My body has become extremely sensitive to numerous things. Loud noises can easily upset me. The moment I buy into the belief that the body or the mind have power over me, I get nervous. The ego driven body feels as if it wants to speed up, but not in a comfortable way. Other times a sleepiness takes over, and I am overwhelmed. Before I understood what was happening, the body was my prison. Foods I used to love don't taste good anymore. My taste buds for sweets can only endure small amounts of the sugars. It seems my body and mind have been turned upside-down.

In the beginning, right after the "Tenth Gate" opening, my sleeping pattern was severely interrupted. Often at night, I observe myself as a small, insignificant being on this planet. We, as in humanity, are but a speck of energy, possessing powerful abilities. Yet, we lay barren on the landscape of Mother Earth. This picture I see of humanity is disturbing to me. In another moment, I get jolted into a different reality, my body becomes a conduit for light. A surge of energy transforms into light inside my super-charged body, penetrating deeply. The light takes over and I lose consciousness. When I come back I can't remember what happened.

My meditation practice has changed. The supreme bliss, which I felt in the body for an extended period of time, has mellowed out. Sensations I feel now are connected to my heart. They are feelings of unconditional love that stream from the heart and soul.

Sitting inside the Gurdwara, euphoria takes over when I see Guruji. Tears of joy flow down my cheeks and there is nothing I can do when this happens, joy overtakes me.

I feel a strange familiarity, as if I have finally come home, after being gone for a very long time. There is a fullness and an emptiness at the same time. But this moment feels rich, like nothing is missing. There is no sadness, and normal earthly things have lost their importance. Then I come back to my full senses and remember where I am.

The practice of loving myself as well as others is like taking a trip on a slow-moving train, but as the locomotive gathers speed I'm not able to jump off, so I simply enjoy the train ride. As the momentum of the train grows, so does the realization that you're on it for the duration. Whatever your end-goal, there is something about the journey that you enjoy.

WHO AM I? WHERE IS GOD?

Life has always been a mystery to me, even when I was six years old. I was told that true wisdom rested outside human understanding. However, everything I ever learned by watching people, and often animals, pointed to grace. Animals, when not threatened, are gracious. I watched a young owl sitting two feet away from me, staring straight into my eyes. There was God right in front of me. This creature was not afraid of me. And vice versa, no need for fear existed in our interaction.

On another occasion I witnessed a unique interaction between a doe and a baby girl who looked like she was about two years old. It was mid- morning at a Northern California resort in the foothills of Napa County. A small herd of deer including the doe gathered near a cabin where the young girl stood watching the deer. The doe approached the youngster and began playfully prancing around the child, lightly touching the youngster's outstretched hand and then playfully backing off as the child moved towards the doe.

This went on for a while when all of a sudden the young girl's mother called for the child to stay away from the startled doe. The doe's mother was also alerted and fetched its young one and the whole family of deer dispersed to safe ground away from the cabin.

Somehow, I knew we all have the power to reach God's wisdom. At a young age, I knew that God is deep inside of every human being.

When I think of God, I think of the current that vibrates in my head. The most profound and easy way to be with God is when I'm about ready to go to sleep. I find myself in a state between waking and not sleeping yet. It is an interesting juncture, and the most glorious and delicious state of existence.

Right before my mind leaves this earth to visit the heavenly plane, there is a period of time that actually leaves a taste of sweetness in my mouth. It's called Amrit. But it's also found when the "Tenth Gate" opens. It can be found only inside the body, when a specific state of awareness is reached. Everything we want is within this deep state of stillness. And therein we find the Ambrosial Nectar or Amrit. And we discover God. Or more preciseley God reveals itself.

CHAPTER 21

THE ENERGY
OF GOD

The day when the "Tenth Gate" opened, my life changed radically. I was able to see God in a different light. I understood the energy of God. However, when the ecstasy wore off, my circuits were blown, I needed to find peace of mind. But I also had to work, raise my child, keep a roof over our head. In other words, there was no peace. I became lost as well as sidetracked for many years.

Everything changed that day after the Kundalini experience. The months and years that followed grew into a downward spiral, life could not get worse. But it did. I became very ill. Sometimes at night when the energy and lights within were pulsating and circling inside my body, I wanted to shut it down, but I couldn't. When I wanted to sleep, I would experience serious bouts of anxiety.

Exhaustion became part of my daily experience but it took a long time to get over it. Sometimes it still happens, but now I accept it, and have learned to handle myself differently. I also recognized that as soon as I bring fear into this encounter, I become exhausted and everything changes. Why was I so afraid of this energy? I needed to learn to accept the emotion of fear and honor it, thus allowing me to let it go.

Fortunately, I was able to overcome those desperate moments of fear and stress. While sitting at the Gurdwara, contemplating, hoping for something to happen, I let my pretensions fall away and it humbled me. The ego had to yield its hold on me, and the resentments towards the world began to dissipate. The wall I had erected around myself prevented me from seeing the bigger picture, I could not see God, no matter how hard I tried.

Then I sat all those years inside the Gurdwara, trying to learn how to get rid of old illusions, how to clear the mind. My ego had to surrender. I had to surrender. I understood that, but I had to get to know my ego better. I had to learn what my ego needed, in order to deliver itself up. Once I got the lessons, it became easy. That's when new energy came flooding in. I dedicated my energy to God. My meditation was deeper than ever. I visited God in the ether. I recognized the Universe with all its glory and spent many hours in God's house. After four years of daily meditation and sitting inside the Gurdwara, Guru Gobind Singh showed up.

A BALANCE STRIKES, TRUST GROWS

Personal preferences that used to matter to me are of no importance now. Before this insight, I would insist on getting my way.

I've learned to let life be my guide. The Universe which I equate with God will give me a deeper insight, enabling me to strike a balance in the way I process matters of importance to me. Kindness goes a long way coupled with thoughtfulness to back it up. When I became aware of trust and will, freedom also became important to me, and this recognition enabled me to honor the freedoms of others that I came in contact with, despite knowing that their views are entirely different from mine.

In this light when we practice the concept of free will as I'm insisting on my will to be done, there is the free will of the other person to consider.

This then is free will - Do what I want, without creating pain for the other. With the "5D" understanding of free will, it motivates me to look at my own behavior in regard to another's free will. First, ego must become the silent onlooker; when ego is mastered and becomes our friend, it will show us the way of discernment.

CHAPTER 22

A NEW ROAD

The road I've traveled after the "Tenth Gate" opened was not easy. What saved me in the beginning was being in silence with myself. Seeing life from a different angle. About two decades later it was Guru Gobind Singh who, in some sense came to my rescue. He brought before me a new understanding of myself. The kindness I experienced with him and his patience is exactly what I needed. The people at the temple also helped me to see a new road.

Within the following pages, I want to reiterate in more detail what it felt like in body and mind to go through the opening of the "Tenth Gate." Not many people have traversed this road before. My wish is for more people who have experienced the "Tenth Gate" opening would be to share their stories and the knowledge they've gathered.

There are more awakenings ahead, more lessons that I gleaned from sitting in meditation, observing people but mostly observing myself.

THE SURPRISE OF DASAM DWAR

It started a couple of days before the actual opening happened. As a matter of fact, I had felt restless for weeks. But on Friday, I could barely contain myself. I was pacing all day and could not find peace even for a moment. I had a feeling as if I was losing my mind and couldn't understand why or what was happening. If I would have gone to the doctor, I believe he would have diagnosed me with a mental illness. It was not only my mind that was affected, but the physical body was also extremely agitated.

What does that mean anyway? These indescribable twitches I felt in my body, surges of energy, and the noises inside, almost drove me insane. People asked if I needed help. What could I answer? I didn't know what my issue was. I was clueless and desperate. The only thing I knew for sure was that I felt out of control. The scariest thought that plagued me for several days, right up to the time when the energy took over was, am I going to survive whatever is happening to me.

At one point I knew I had to give in. Two days later on Sunday evening I had a feeling as if I was experiencing a severe panic attack. I was breathing heavily, with a sensation of doom inside my solar plexus. I decided I couldn't fight my mind or my body any longer. I laid down, closed my eyes and gave myself over to God.

My insides began to roar - I can only describe the noise - as if all of Niagara Falls were hitting me at once, and a great pressure inside my body welled up. A loud hissing sound rumbled from deep inside. The noise was so powerful, I lost my hearing to the outside. Light streamed in front of my closed eyes. I lost my outside senses, but inside with closed eyes, I could see light, felt pressure, and continued to hear the intense roaring and hissing.

That was my initiation (and ironically, it was splendid for a moment) and it lasted thirty-six hours. All the magical, magnificent senses coming together in front of my mind's eye: ecstasy shooting up my spine, filling every cell of my body. This was a gigantic force of energy pulsating through my body, filling me up with white light.

RIGHT AFTER THE RAPTURE

Right after the opening, while still in rapture, the top of my head felt as if someone had placed a cup of ice inside the skull. I became hypersensitive. Inside my mind, I was watching an endless place of what I can only describe as the Universe, looking out into creation, as I sit and watch on the edge. This was a mind-bending experience. I have never experienced a light like this before. It was brighter than a hundred suns, and slowly it illuminated and took over my whole being.

Even years after, my head needed covering when the wind blew cold, the pain was uncomfortable. To this day, I do not like when my head is touched on the crown. It's still sensitive, a feeling of coolness and a slight breeze still moves around on top.

Sensitivity to almost everything became my new normal. Honesty impels me to admit, that I had to desensitize myself by eating junk food, drinking alcohol, and distracting myself by being constantly around people. My close friends could not understand what was going on at that time. They could see my exhaustion, but there was no way to explain what went on in my body or mind to others. Life was gloomy, with too many side roads leading only to more misery; earthly attachments only created more pain. For the longest time it seemed, there was no escape from the hell I lived in.

HELL ON EARTH

At times when life seemed unbearable and overwhelming, all I could do was to sit in a corner and cry. Having to raise a young child, I can't remember how I got through it. The highs were high, but the lows seemed like a pit in the darkness. During those periods, often resting in bed, praying and looking up, I would ask, "Why am I being punished?" I wondered if God had forsaken me.

More than once I found myself in such pain wondering if this was a heart attack. To this day I wonder if that pounding in my chest left permanent damage to my heart. My nervous system was incredibly overwhelmed. I felt death would have been a relief.

How can one experience the Universe with its splendor and then fall back down to hell? How is that possible? I was losing control, not only of my body, but my life was unfocused, which later turned out to be exactly what I needed.

My body felt as if I had been stuck in a light socket, spun around in the spin cycle of a washing machine and then spit out to dry. The energy had completely and utterly drained me. Due to the agitation caused by the Kundalini experience I had temporarily lost control of my body. The mind with ego helped me to cope with the fears, which I had developed, while hanging on to old belief systems and old ways of behavior. After the "Tenth Gate" opened, familiar things that used to give me security before, fell away. My world crashed, and it continued for nearly eight years.

ACCEPTANCE

The power to gain control is the letting go of it. It's the opposite of what I thought. The harder I gripped on to fear, the greater the pain became. Eventually, the wisdom of letting go of control presented itself. Because I was overwhelmed emotionally, I had no energy left. I was forced by my own body to give up, to collapse into exhaustion. This forced me to give up control. Then I began trusting my instinct and intuition. It was the beginning of a little freedom. More insights were to follow.

The determination I developed of gaining insights as to what this super-charged energy was, became my mission, my life path. Unbeknownst to me, the path led directly to Guru Gobind Singh.

This path liberated me to seek deep truths about myself. It helped me to see the soul of humanity, which eventually lead to God and my higher power. That turned out to be a long and arduous journey, over many decades, since the opening of the "Tenth Gate."

The high point of the journey began when I saw Guru Gobind Singh. At that time, I had no understanding of what was happening. I was stunned at first, later dumbfounded, because I had no idea who was in front of me, or how to receive such a blessing.

THE PATH TO ENLIGHTENMENT

Getting to know God has always been my highest inspiration. The "Tenth Gate" was the vehicle that unblocked all my fears, and anxieties about my perceived disfunctions. What I concluded after being in misery for a few years, was the fact that I felt tired of being in the darkness. What I didn't know, in order to see the light, I had to be in darkness. The Kundalini experience helped me to appreciate that the process I went through to see the light, allowed me to see the darkness first. The "Tenth Gate" is not enlightenment itself, but a guiding light leading to eventual enlightenment.

Yes, there is the light, the bliss and the whole universe laying at my feet. This question arose almost one year after the opening of my crown:

"What do I do now?"

The time it took for my body to settle into a new awareness, and in understanding what happened to me, required a great deal of strength. The one thing that I could retreat to and enjoyed tremendously is the void. It is a space that finds me during deep meditation. There I sit in the silence with the splendor of the Universe, which I came to know so intimately.

To keep my body and mind from falling apart, I would sit within the void. For years that had to be enough. That's the only thing I could muster with some excitement. Everything else was difficult and painful.

Soon after seeing Guru Gobind Singh, I felt like a big push was coming, so I asked during meditation: "What is this space where nothing exists, while losing feeling within my whole body? Is it like death of the physical body?"

The answer came unexpectedly. It felt as if I was taken deeper into the space of the void. To my surprise, there is a deeper void. Within seconds I understood. The space before the deep void is where I used to spend most of my meditation time, where the Supreme Soul merges in this space with all souls. And you're still aware of it. But in this deep space, senses do not exist. Only light exists, then that disappears too.

In the deepest of spaces, the experience is of death; not in the sense of physically dying, but in a nanosecond, you know you're leaving. The body and mind are left behind, there I have no memory. Coming back from this place, in the big picture of things, I knew that the individual is but a speck of energy. Not less, not more.

The whole idea of souls merging as one with the Universe is a concept that I am now beginning to fully comprehend. It dawned on me because from a firsthand experience from many years ago.

CHAPTER 23

THE EXPERIENCE OF DYING

As a six-year-old, I had drowned and was declared dead by a lifeguard. I listened to his declaration while I watched from above. Within seconds I was back in my body, and back to the physical experience we call life. Here was a turning point, which I only recognized later in life. But in the meantime, I had forgotten about the drowning until I was a bit older.

My god mother whom I called Aunty, reminded me during a visit to her house on a summer vacation, when I was fourteen. She told me of the drowning at Stausee, a man-made lake near my hometown in Germany, where we used to go swimming.

"When you're older and want to know the story, I will tell you," she told me. Unfortunately, she passed before I had a chance to talk to her about the drowning. Later, at twenty-eight, I nearly drowned again. From that second incident, nightmares of my death by drowning at Stausee occurred nightly.

THE WAKE-UP CALL, FIRST TIME AROUND

What the nightmares brought back into my memory was the moments of dying. I saw myself being under the water, my knees bent under, leaning against a cement wall. Unable to move, my feet and legs locked underneath me. I remember looking up, seeing the reflected light of the sunshine distorted by the waves of the lake. Then after a moment of darkness, I came back to my senses, and entered a dark gray cloud-like portal gate. In a blink of the eye, I exited the cloud into a sun-drenched and beautiful meadow, surrounded by lots of tall Kelly green pine trees and bright colorful vegetation.

To my surprise there were people whom I knew, especially my grandfather, Opa, who greeted me with wonder. I recognized other family members who died years ago. I heard unspoken words from Opa: "What are you doing here?" He communicated telepathically to me, "You can't stay!"

I gazed at him as he took my hand in his and we walked on a path towards the other end of the meadow. There a person walked out of the same kind of cloud portal I had come from on the other end. The man took my hand from Opa's, and we turned around and walked back to the cloud portal. As I took a good look around, I loved this place, with its beautiful flowers and a bench to sit on right next to a tall tree. The scenery was very inviting. However, the man holding my hand was firm. He counseled me, "It is not your time yet. You have to go back, it is not your time."

And with that statement he guided me back through the cloud from which I entered this wondrous place. The being who walked me back manifested a palpable spirit of gentle kindness that overwhelmed me with complete serenity.

After going back through the cloud portal, I found myself hovering in the air, slightly above a tall pole. As I looked down below me, there were lots of people, my god mother, her son Peter, and a man who said, "She is dead. There is nothing I can do."

My Aunty was crying. The only person paying attention to me was Peter, who knelt next to me.

When I heard the man say, "She is dead," I looked down at the crowd and thought, "No way! I'm not dead!"

Quickly, accompanied by a swooshing-like sound, I was back in my body. Peter, still kneeling by my side looked at me as I opened my eyes. He was astonished and tried to tell his mother, but she wouldn't hear of it until I took a deep breath and started coughing.

THE SECOND TIME AROUND

My second near-drowning episode was much harder than the first. I had night terrors for weeks, often waking up from some terrible nightmare drenched in a cold sweat. I watched myself reliving the fear of dying. Time seemed endless, and I felt as though my entire life was passing in front of my eyes, while paddling water underneath me to stay afloat. It was getting dark, and breathing was getting harder. In a panic, I wanted to scream, but something told me, "Hold on, you are alright, just hold on." My heart was beating so hard, I felt the pulse in my neck. My chest cavity was pounding in terror.

As the sun descended over the gray and cold lake, I could barely see the sailboat coming around to save me. Every time they made a pass, I couldn't reach my husband's stretched-out hand from the side of the boat. The wind was too strong, the waves were too choppy to maneuver steadily, and I was getting weaker by the minute. This was the worst fear I had ever lived through. In a panic I was close to losing my life, but something saved me from myself.

In this big lake, there was a voice that spoke and said, "Hold on! You're almost there, you're not dying here." After four passes the boat finally came close enough before a hand pulled me out of the water. When my husband's hand grabbed mine, I did not let go. Our two friends who were sailing with us were relieved to see me sitting safely in the boat. We all cried after I was pulled inside.

My husband was stunned. I had a feeling that he didn't think I was coming home that night. No one talked on the way back to the boat ramp. This was a very close call. The shock and exhaustion were written over all our faces.

This event was an important catapult that woke me up, pushed me into pursuing a spiritual path. That journey is still going on. After having had the "Tenth Gate" opening a few years after this incident, gave me the needed strength I would come to rely on in my life.

I prayed hard that evening while trying to keep my head above the choppy water of the lake. I made a promise to God. Then came the "voice" that helped me to make the commitment and passion to follow the narrow path towards my spiritual development. I knew there would be freedom near the end, but never realized what that meant or what was specifically required of me to accomplish it.

Now, after years traversing this path, I understand the freedom I gained by taking on this arduous yet fulfilling journey. I walk with trust and dedication to a higher wisdom, and devotion to God. The rewards have grown into compassion, self-love, soul wisdom, detachment from earthly things, high self-esteem, mindful behavior and thoughtfulness. Also, commitment to seeing projects through to the end, while my faith is unshakeable, and trusting in my intuition. The senses I've acquired expand beyond worldly imagination.

I can speak with authority of realms I have visited, and of encounters with masters from different spheres. Having witnessed powerful and unexplainable energies at work, I've undertaken the most significant and extensive journey of my life. The experiences I gathered are footprints of my spiritual evolution.

What we get from life is defined by our experiences. With these experiences, there comes a point when the student becomes the teacher. They propel us into different levels by making us aware to look at life through the eyes of the beloved. If we are so fortunate to become aware that the world with its inhabitants become our brothers and sisters who are unconditionally loved, we can be open to the idea that all people are conduits for spiritual messages, and they will present to us what we need to learn.

CHAPTER 24

WISDOM GAINED

Frequently, it feels as if I'm living in two worlds. The materialistic world, where everything has its proper description, everything has its place. I have explained to people about Kundalini and the energy it brings. Most do not understand and can't relate to it. I understand. Before I had this experience of the opening of the "Tenth Gate," I would have thought myself a bit off balance too. But the Holy Book of the Sikh religion, the "Guru Grant Sahib" describes these things to the fullest degree. That gave me a measure of validation and hope. I gained new insights and wisdom.

It had taken many years before the worst of my depression and the weakness within my body got better. I decided I had enough of not feeling well. My body and mind needed a change, but my spirit needed a new way of seeing life, too. Slowly I began to meditate again. That made the difference. I learned how to get deep into the light and into the void.

That's my Universe during meditation. I'm in the vacuum. It is illuminated by the light and by nothingness. I am transformed by the energy and the opening of the "Tenth Gate," which gave me a characteristically hypersensitive consciousness. My visions are heavenly and luminous.

It doesn't mean that I am not sad or upset. However, my perceptions have changed. With a different view of life, whenever I'm in a moment of sadness, I accept it and then think about it for a moment or two. After that the sadness is part of my past. Nothing is of paramount importance anymore.

My mind is satisfied with its inner life. The light shines brightly within, and when issues need to be addressed, the mind can step away and let the wisdom of the Universe take over. This is the treasure.

EXPERIENCING THE VOID

Being focused, quiet and open, the perfect time to tune into nothingness is now. The focus in deep meditation becomes the void. We allow it to take us deep into our own nature, to the treasure of the life beyond the core of what is called existence. Here lies the power of changing our world. The mind steps away and makes room for the greater wisdom. All records are kept within this realm. Everything is known here. "Absolute Knowledge" resides here. Humanity's divinity is experienced here while merging with the Universe.

From this space, the mind emerges with a changed vision, altered in perception, as the body has no choice but to follow and change form on the deepest level. All that has ever existed and will ever exist is known here. Everything is important. At the same time, everything becomes nothing.

It started with an intention and grew into something that took on its own life and here we are. What began as intentional meditation, deep breathing, and yoga, the "Tenth Gate" opening revealed unexpected, powerful, amazing, and life changing results.

After many years of difficulty, my devotional practice was not in vain. It was only possible after I had given up my ego that I could see how ego was my protector, but only my wounded child needed healing. The surrender was sweet. Ego is my friend. My mind could finally be silent.

That's when Guru Gobind Singh showed up.

When I asked him: "Guru I can see you. Guru, I can hear you. Guru, why are you speaking to me?"

He answered back: "Because you listen."

I was willing to listen. I was willing to hear. The connection to God and my higher self became strong and is now unbreakable. I am not moving away from God and will not lose consciousness again.

Are you ready? It may take a minute or a lifetime to the devotion of God, allowing yourself to merge with that energy, experiencing bliss. Are you willing to examine yourself and the world around you? Do you want freedom from earthly shackle? The wisdom is yours.

The words that are written in italics are from the Holy Book of the Sikh religion, the "Sacred Nitnem." Also, some italicized passages are Hymns that I copied at the Temple during Sunday services.

For more information or classes on meditation, as well as speaking engagements, please feel free to contact Karin Vastola by e-mail: Karinvastola7@gmail.com. On most days you will find Karin Vastola at the Gurdwara, Sikh Temple, in her home town in Northern California.

The art work on the cover was done by my friend, Michael Valdez, a great artist and also my editor. I am so grateful for his work and effort he made to help me to get this book published.

Copyright 2020 by Karin Vastola.

All rights reserved. No part of this publication may be copied, reproduced, stored in any retrieval system, transmitted or utilized in any form or by any means, electronic, mechanical, photocopying, recording or otherwise, without the expressed permission of the author.

Requests must be addressed in writing to:
Karin Vastola
P.O. Box 5442
Marysville, CA 95901

Printed in the United States
By Bookmasters